T0024281

Praise for *The Laws of Wealth*

"When I'm looking for sharp, against-the-grain insights on how we can and should make better investing decisions, I always turn to Daniel Crosby. If he's publishing, blogging, or tweeting, I want to know about it. It also doesn't hurt that he's often hilarious in taking our built-in foibles and creating the potential for ending up in a much better place than we would otherwise. This book is yet another fantastic contribution to the practice of sound (and sane) investing."

**Brian Portnoy, Founder of Shaping Wealth
& Author, *The Geometry of Wealth***

"Individual investors are often their own worst enemies, whether they're selling when they should be buying, focusing on their stocks' day-to-day swings or letting the media drive them into a panicked emotional state. In Dr. Daniel Crosby's newest book, he breaks down how to implement a set of easy-to-follow rules to keep investors on track. Don't let your mind ruin your investing outcomes. Read his book and arm yourself against yourself today."

LouAnn Lofton, The Motley Fool

"Dr. Daniel Crosby is one of the preeminent behavioral psychologists in investing today, and it shows with this tour de force of how an investor can manage their wealth. With these few simple rules, investors can easily build a framework allowing them to thrive, even when their human instincts try to sabotage their investing. Get this book!"

Aaron Klein, CEO at Riskalyze

"The financial services industry is broken and has for too long ignored the human factor. Savvy investors and advisors understand that emotions, decisions and behavior are at least as important as big returns and Dr. Daniel Crosby explains just that in *The Laws of Wealth*."

David Geller, CEO, GV Financial

"Drawing the connection that what makes us interesting as humans can make us unsuccessful at managing our money in times of turbulence, Dr. Crosby provides a safe haven with his framework for success. This book is not only informative but enjoyable, as he gently exposes how human behavior impacts our decision making."

Noreen D. Beaman, CEO of Brinker Capital, Inc

"Using lively and engaging real-life examples Dr. Crosby gives insights into innate human behavior and its role within the financial markets. In this entertaining book he provides a brilliant invaluable practical framework for investors, financial professionals and anyone in search of true wealth."

Dr. Svetlana Gherzi, Behavioral Finance Specialist, UBS

"Step away from CNBC and into financial therapy! People often think that 'buy low, sell high' is the first (and only) rule of investing. This deceptively simple phrase motivates most, if not all investors, and yet many investors fail to successfully follow this simple mantra. In *The Laws of Wealth*, Daniel Crosby explains why we struggle with deceptively simple investment decisions, suggesting that first rule of profitable investing is to get out of your own way."

Meredith A. Jones, Author, *Women of The Street:*
Why Female Money Managers Generate Higher Returns
(And How You Can Too)

𝒯𝒽𝑒 LAWS 𝑜𝑓 WEALTH

Educated at Brigham Young and Emory Universities, Dr. Daniel Crosby is a psychologist, behavioral finance expert and asset manager who applies his study of market psychology to everything from financial product design to security selection. He is co-author of the *New York Times* bestseller *Personal Benchmark: Integrating Behavioral Finance and Investment Management* and founder of Nocturne Capital. He is at the forefront of behavioralizing finance. His ideas have appeared in the Huffington Post and Risk Management Magazine, as well as his monthly columns for WealthManagement.com and Investment News.

Daniel was named one of the "12 Thinkers to Watch" by Monster.com, a "Financial Blogger You Should Be Reading" by AARP and in the "Top 40 Under 40" by Investment News.

When he is not consulting around market psychology, Daniel enjoys independent films, fanatically following St. Louis Cardinals baseball, and spending time with his wife and three children.

Also by Daniel Crosby

Everyone You Love Will Die

*Personal Benchmark: Integrating Behavioral Finance
and Investment Management (with Chuck Widger)*

The Behavioral Investor

The
LAWS
of
WEALTH

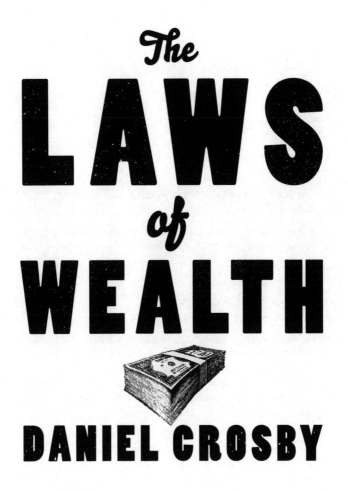

DANIEL CROSBY

HARRIMAN HOUSE LTD
3 Viceroy Court
Bedford Road
Petersfield
Hampshire
GU32 3LJ
GREAT BRITAIN
Tel: +44 (0)1730 233870

Email: enquiries@harriman-house.com
Website: harriman.house

First published in Great Britain in 2016. This paperback edition 2021.
Copyright © Daniel Crosby

The right of Daniel Crosby to be identified as the Author has been asserted in accordance with the Copyright, Design and Patents Act 1988.

Paperback ISBN: 978-0-85719-783-2
eBook ISBN: 978-0-85719-784-9

British Library Cataloguing in Publication Data
A CIP catalogue record for this book can be obtained from the British Library.

For
Katrina, Charlotte, Liam, Lola,
and the three angels
– all that matters

Every owner of a physical copy of this edition of

can download the eBook for free direct from us at Harriman House, in a DRM-free format that can be read on any eReader, tablet or smartphone.

Simply head to:

ebooks.harriman-house.com/lawsofwealthpbk

to get your copy now.

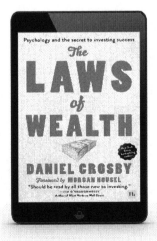

Acknowledgements

It has been appropriately noted that it takes a village to raise a child and the same can be said of writing a book. This book exists because of these people and their contributions to my life:

Alison Crosby—life and a love of writing

Philip Crosby—an unrivaled career counselor

Nana—for squash casserole, sweet potatoes and turnip greens

Karl Farnsworth—the biggest fan of my books

Hege Farnsworth—for raising an unbelievable daughter

Ali McCarthy—for 'buying low' and giving me a career

Chuck Widger—guidance, patience and a roadmap

Craig Pearce—for the opportunity

Jim Lake—motivation, energy and purpose

Stephanie Giaramita—humor, wit and hip-hop

Brinker Capital—for providing me with a work family

Steve Wruble—dreaming, scheming and backtesting

Edmond Walters—mentorship, opportunity and candor

Tim McCabe—encouragement and Southern hospitality

Meredith Jones—tireless guidance and patience with my quirks

Brian Portnoy—for not suffering fools

Maddie Quinlan—for proofreading, eh!

John Nolan—wisdom, humor and bagels

Peter Kalianiotis—for telling me that I wasn't charging enough

Jordan Hutchison—for believing in The Dynasty

Corey Hoffstein—for explaining how the world works

Noreen Beaman—for being a leader

Leslie Hadad and Rachel Barrow—for the early support

To the thousands of people who have watched me speak, purchased my books or given me an encouraging word—your support has blessed my life.

Contents

Foreword by Morgan Housel

Think of how big the world is.

Now think of how good animals are at hiding.

Now think about a biologist whose job it is to determine whether a species has gone extinct.

Not an easy thing to do, is it?

A group of Australian biologists once discovered something remarkable. More than a third of all mammals deemed extinct in the last 500 years have later been rediscovered, alive.

It's an example of something we don't think about enough: A lot of what we know in science is bound to change. That's what makes science great, what makes it work, and what distinguishes it from religion. Science is filled with rules, evidence-based theories, and probabilistic observations. But laws—immutable truths lacking exceptions—are rare. Most fields only have a handful.

But the handful of laws that do exist play a special role. They're the great grandmothers, the old wise men, of the day-to-day theories and rules used to discover a new truth. There's a hierarchy of science: laws at the bottom, specific rules above that, then theories, observations, hunches, and so on. The higher you go on the pyramid the more exciting things become. That's where discovery and opportunity live. But everything at the top of the pyramid must respect the laws at the bottom.

The idea of flexible rules deriving from unshakeable laws applies to every field. John Reed writes in his book *Succeeding*:

When you first start to study a field, it seems like you have to memorize a zillion things. You don't. What you need is to identify the core principles that govern the field. The million things you thought you had to memorize are simply various combinations of the core principles.

It's the same thing with our money.

You can't accurately describe how complicated the global economy is. There are more than 200,000,000 businesses in the world. Three-hundred trillion dollars of financial assets. Eighty trillion dollars of GDP. Almost 200 countries, thousands of cultures and norms. With seven billion people, a rough calculation shows there's about two tons of pure serotonin careening through the global economy at every moment.

Wrapping your head around the global economy—predicting recessions, bubbles, GDP growth and the like—is nearly impossible. There are too many moving parts.

Consider a few points:

There are, as I write this, something like 630,00 publicly traded companies in the world.

There are four times as many mutual funds and ETFs than there are Starbucks locations in the world (114,131 vs. 29,324).

About the same number of people were awarded bachelor's degrees in 2010 as filed for personal bankruptcy (1.6 million).

Between 1980 and 2014, 40% of U.S. stocks lost at least 70% of their value and never recovered.

40% of Americans can't come up with $400 in an emergency.

78% of workers live paycheck to paycheck.

46.1% of Americans die with less than $10,000 in assets.

From 1950 to 2018, the S&P 500 rose 151-fold but was only positive on 52% of days.

It's just incomprehensible.

But we try—desperately—to comprehend it with financial models, spreadsheets, graphs, and predictions.

There's nothing wrong with attempting to do so. Yet when we try to make sense of the financial world we must always remember that the crazy, dynamic parts of finance are governed by just a few laws.

Like most fields, there aren't many financial laws. But they are what matter most. The more you study finance the more you see that all the crazy and complex parts of the economy are really just variations on a few critical points.

In *The Laws of Wealth*, Daniel Crosby does not answer the questions, "How do I get rich?" or "Where should I invest my money?" Instead, he lays out the base principles necessary to answer those questions— questions that vary from person to person, country to country, and generation to generation, yet always governed by a few laws.

Russian novelist Fyodor Dostoyevsky once wrote of natural laws:
Nature does not ask your permission, she has nothing to do with your wishes, and whether you like her laws or dislike them, you are bound to accept her as she is, and consequently all her conclusions.

So it goes with every field's laws, including finance.

Morgan Housel
The Collaborative Fund

Preface or: How I Learned to Stop Worrying and Read this Book

GENTLE READER, THIS book was crafted with the singular purpose of making you wealthier. This wealth, if it is to be realized, will be hard won. It will require you to exercise patience, admit your own flaws and assent to the idea that a few simple rules are the best hope you have for managing your self and your wealth. Given that you, as a member of the human family, have tendencies toward impatience, arrogance and a fetish for complexity, it is very likely that you will screw this up. Nevertheless, this book's purpose remains.

My efforts to save you from yourself are divided into two parts:

- **Part One**—An explication of the rules necessary for managing oneself along the journey of compounding wealth. I present ten commandments based on hundreds of years of market history, rooted in the truism that at all times, you control what matters most (i.e., your behavior).
- **Part Two**—Sets forth a rule-based approach to behavioral investing (henceforth, RBI). Part Two can be conceptualized as a funnel that moves from generality to specificity and from risk management to return generation. It begins by suggesting a universe of behavioral risk which leads directly into a conversation of a rule-based investment

approach that mitigates said risk. It ends with a discussion of the five specific factors I consider within my RBI approach, provided as an example of potential applications.

To help you narrow in on the practical applications of what has been covered, I include 'What now?' summaries at the end of each chapter. These summaries will point you towards what you should think, ask and do to take advantage of the lessons learned and put them into practice to improve your investing.

I make the case that the rules governing the world of an investor are much different than those dominant elsewhere in life. Our success in the market is contingent on working to the rules of the market and this in turn depends on us knowing ourselves. It is my hope that reading this book will leave you both financially better off and with a richer awareness of self.

Introduction:
Of Worms & Wealth

"Psychology seems to lie behind all the ways that potentially improve stock market returns."

—**Ben Stein and Phil DeMuth,**
The Little Book of Alternative Investments

Of guinea worms...

THE AMERICAN SOUTH is a proud and sometimes troubled region that is distinctive by virtue of its unique foodways, unmistakable accent, and reputation for both interpersonal and climatic warmth. I am a son of this strange and wonderful place, a native Alabaman who now lives in the de facto Capital of the South, Atlanta.

Atlanta is many things: home to two Nobel Peace Prize winners (Martin Luther King, Jr. and Jimmy Carter), the only American city to burn to the ground twice and the host of the 1996 Summer Olympic Games. But perhaps most impressive of all, Atlanta is the world's epicenter of epidemiological research, thanks to the Centers for Disease Control and Prevention (CDC) and the Carter Center.

The CDC boasts over 14,000 employees in 50 countries and is the tip of the spear for fighting infectious diseases domestically and internationally. The Carter Center, the philanthropic legacy of American president Jimmy Carter, has as its motto the ambitious goal of "Waging Peace. Fighting Disease. Building Hope."

Although both organizations are constantly diligent, their work tends to enter public consciousness only around high profile health events like the HIV/AIDS epidemic, SARS, avian flu, Ebola and, more recently, COVID-19. As a result of headline-grabbing illnesses with dramatic names (I'm looking at you, Mad Cow Disease) taking a disproportionate share of the limelight, some of these organizations' most impactful programs go largely unheralded. One such campaign is the Guinea worm eradication effort headed up by Dr. Donald Hopkins.

To understand the full import of the work done by Dr. Hopkins and his team at the Carter Center, we must first undertake the (somewhat unpleasant) task of understanding the ill effects wrought by the parasite Dracunculus medinensis, or Guinea worm as it is more commonly known. The Guinea worm is the largest tissue parasite impacting humans and can grow to over three feet in length. Guinea worms are reproductively adept as well, with the adult female carrying an incredible three million embryos! The World Health Organization notes that, "the parasite migrates through the victim's subcutaneous tissues causing severe pain especially when it occurs in the joints. The worm eventually emerges (from the feet in most cases), causing an intensely painful oedema, a blister and an ulcer accompanied by fever, nausea and vomiting." Ouch.

To complicate matters, the very means by which this horrific pain can be abated actually furthers the transmission of the parasite. Seeking respite from the pain, sufferers run to their local water source and submerge their worm-ridden limbs in a desperate attempt at relief. The immediate result to the victim is positive—she receives some cooling of the impacted area and short-term symptomatic relief. But the succor of one individual comes at the expense of many, as the Guinea worm now finds itself in water, its preferred site for reproduction. As you have probably now guessed, the parasites multiply in the water, which is then passed on to thirsty villagers who eventually become infected and return to the water source for relief, perpetuating the cycle.

But the negative societal sequelae of the parasite are far greater than just the physical pain it causes (easy for me to say). The book, *Influencer: The Power to Change Anything*, describes the fallout thusly:

"Sufferers cannot work their crops for many weeks. When parents are afflicted, their children may drop out of school to help out with chores. Crops cannot be cultivated. The harvest is lost. Starvation ensues. The cycle of illiteracy and poverty consumes the next generation. Often, secondary infections caused by the worm can kill. Consequently, for over 3,500 years the Guinea worm has been a major barrier to economic and social progress in dozens of nations."[1]

It should be abundantly clear by now that when Dr. Hopkins and his team declared war on the Guinea worm in 1986, they went into battle against a formidable foe. But their battle plan was not what most expected. Rather than focus their efforts on a medicinal cure for the ailment, they sought to change the human behavior that propagates its spread. In so doing they have done what many thought impossible— they have nearly eradicated a disease for which there is no cure.

The way they achieved this improbable success was by doing something highly intuitive: they examined the uninfected villages, noted a small number of vital behaviors, and publicized their findings broadly. In specific (and in case you ever find yourself in a developing country), the vital behaviors were as follows:

Villagers in healthy villages showed a willingness to speak up when a friend, family member or neighbor became infected. The infected people were kept far away from the communal water source at the height of their pain (i.e., as the worms were emerging from the skin).

By codifying these two crucial actions and informing others of their power, Dr. Hopkins and his team impacted the physical, mental and economic wellbeing of millions. The tremendous scope of their work belies the simplicity of the solution; nothing they had done to rid the world of this scourge was especially groundbreaking. Dr. Hopkins just understood the power of a few important behaviors, broadly and consistently applied.

...and big returns

The parallels between your wealth and a tropical parasite may seem too remote (or too disgusting) to consider, but there is in fact a great deal we can learn from the eradication of the Guinea worm. First, we must own up to the reality that we investors are afflicted with a disease for which there is not, nor will ever be, a cure. That disease is our own fear and greed. My hope is that by the time you have completed this book, you will be as convinced as I am that psychology presents both the biggest impediment to satisfactory investment returns and your greatest source of potential advantage over other, less-disciplined investors.

Second, you must accept that the only way to eradicate the disease of fear and greed is through disciplined adherence to a set of vital behaviors. Just as could be said of the behaviors that freed the villagers, the behaviors set forth here are simple and intuitive to grasp but gut-wrenchingly painful to execute. Is it simple to grasp intellectually that one ought not to approach the water supply when afflicted with a parasite? Of course. Is it easy to do when your body is ablaze with pain? No way.

Likewise, the ideas you will encounter in this book in a moment of cool calculation are likely to engender vigorous head nodding. But your ability to execute them in a disciplined fashion in all market conditions will determine their efficacy. A villager who knows not to stick his foot in the water and does it anyway is no better off than the clueless villager, and so it goes for investors. Just like the villagers, it is only as we learn to endure a painful today for the promise of a better tomorrow that we will become truly skilled investors.

Moving beyond biases

It seems to be human nature to be fascinated by pathology. Sigmund Freud began his study of the human psyche by outlining how it was broken (hint: your Mom) and the discipline of psychoanalysis continued down that path for over a century. It was roughly 150 years before the study of clinical psychology was offset at all by the study of what we now call positive psychology—the study of what makes us happy, strong and exceptional.

Perhaps it is no surprise then that behavioral finance too began with the study of the anomalous and is only now coming around to a more solution-focused ideal. While a thorough review of the transition from efficient to behavioral approaches isn't why we are here, it's worth considering the rudiments of these ideas and how we can improve upon them.

For decades, the prevailing economic theories espoused a view of Economic Man as rational, utility maximizing and self-interested. On these simple (if unrealistic) assumptions, economists built mathematical models of exceeding elegance but limited real-world applicability. It all worked beautifully, until it didn't. Goaded by a belief in the predictability of Economic Man, The Smartest People in the Room picked up pennies in front of steamrollers—until they got flattened.

On the strength of hedge fund implosions, multiple manias with accompanying crashes and mounting evidence of human irrationality, Economic Man began to give way to Irrational Man. Behavioral proponents begin to document the flaws of investors with the same righteous zeal proponents of market efficiency had previously adopted to defend the aggregate wisdom of the crowd. At my last count, psychologists and economists had documented 117 biases capable of obscuring lucid financial decision-making. *One hundred and seventeen* different ways for you to get it wrong.

The problem with all of this Ivory Tower philosophizing is that none of it truly helps investors. For a clinical psychologist, a diagnosis is a necessary but far from sufficient part of a treatment plan. No shrink worth his $200 an hour would label you pathological and show you the door, yet that is largely what behavioral finance has given the investing public: a surfeit of pathology and a dearth of solutions.

To consider firsthand the futility of being told only what not to do, let's try a simple exercise.

"Do not think of a pink elephant."

What happened as you read the sentence above? Odds are, you did the very thing I asked you not to do and imagined a pink elephant. How disappointing! You could have imagined any number of things—you had infinity minus one options—and yet you still disobeyed my simple request. Oh well, I haven't given up on you yet. Let's try one more time.

"Do not, whatever you do, imagine a large purple elephant with a parasol daintily tiptoeing across a high wire connecting two tall buildings in a large metropolitan area."

You did it again, didn't you?

What you just experienced was the very natural tendency to imagine and even ruminate on something, even when you know you oughtn't. Consider the person on a diet who has created a lengthy list of bad foods. He may, for instance, repeat the mantra, "I will not eat a cookie, I will not eat a cookie, I will not eat a cookie," any time he experiences the slightest temptation.

But what is the net effect of all of his self-flagellating rumination? Effectively he has thought about cookies all day and is likely to cave at the first sign of an Oreo. The research is unequivocal that a far more effective approach is to reorient that behavior into something desirable rather than repeat messages of self-denial that ironically keep the evil object top of mind.

Unfortunately for investors, up until now there have been far more histrionic "Don't do this!" messages than constructive "Do this insteads." My aim is to redress the balance and provide you with concrete suggestions for managing both your behavior and your money.

Beyond "Just say no"

Not only do negativity and self-shaming fail to bring about the desired behavior; sometimes they shut down proactivity altogether. The leaders of VitalSmarts—innovators in corporate training and leadership development—share just such a story in their work, *Influencer: The Power to Change Anything*. They tell the story of King Rama IX of Thailand, who on the occasion of his 60th birthday decided to enact an historic show of his largesse. His gift? He chose to grant amnesty to over 30,000 prisoners.

The year was 1988 and heretofore, the HIV/AIDS virus in Thailand had largely been contained to the prison system. But with the release of tens of thousands of prisoners into a country with a thriving sex trade, that changed quickly. Within 365 days, as many as one-third of the sex workers in certain provinces were found to be HIV positive. With sad predictability, married men soon began contracting the disease from prostitutes, bringing it back to the suburbs and their unsuspecting partners. With over one million Thais already infected and nearly 1% of the population working in the sex trade, the projections for future rates of infection were horrifying.

In response, the government convened a task force led by one Dr. Wiwat. He was charged, effectively, with scaring the people straight. He and his team created dramatic scare pieces with tag lines like, "The dreaded plague is coming!" But when they checked on their progress a few years later, they found that their "scared straight" campaign actually had negative utility. The problem was getting worse, so they decided to take a new tack.

Dr. Wiwat and his team first pinpointed the root of the problem: 97% of all new HIV infections came from sex with prostitutes. This information focused Wiwat on the source—he must convince Thailand's sex workers to insist on using condoms. Where fear had once ruled, education now took hold. Vague scare tactics were replaced with useful tips on how to procure, engage and dispose of prophylactics. By the late 1990s, five million Thais who ought to have had AIDS did not, given Dr. Wiwat's pivot to outcomes-based information over fear mongering. Whether discussing pink elephants or Thai hookers, the result is the same—shame and fear are poor motivators of good behavior and can even lead to a paradoxical reaction.

As further evidence of the effect of priming on behavior, in *Predictably Irrational* Dan Ariely shows that performance on a math test varied depending on whether women were reminded that they were Asian (stereotypically viewed as being good at math) or a woman (stereotypically viewed as being bad at math). As you've surely guessed, those primed to think of themselves as Asian outperformed those primed to consider their femininity.

Likewise, Meir Statman shares research on socioeconomic labels and spending behavior in his book *What Investors Really Want*. Participants who were primed to think of themselves as poor were far more likely to spend their money on conspicuous luxury goods, a marker of wealth to the outside world. In both cases, the behavior of participants was manipulated by a reminder of the box in which they fit. They were told where they belonged and they acted accordingly.

Following this through in the world of investing, such mental priming, as it is known, is dangerous. By emphasizing the behavioral faults that beset investors—and without providing constructive alternative approaches—behavioral finance has primed investors to fall foul of these biases and engage in behavior that makes the problem worse.

Investors are not the self-interested, utility maximizing drones the efficient market brigade once thought, and neither are they the Homer-Simpson-esque dolts they have more recently been painted as.

Instead of ever-longer lists of ways in which they are flawed, investors need a realistic understanding of their strengths and weaknesses, as well as concrete advice for magnifying the former and minimizing the latter. Just like a wise Thai doctor, I hope this book will scare you enough that you pay attention, but provide you with positive direction to avoid the dreaded plague of investor misbehavior.

Michel de Montaigne said it far more elegantly:

"I feel grateful to the Milesian wench who, seeing the philosopher
Thales continually spending his time in contemplation of the
heavenly vault and always keeping his eyes raised upward, put
something in his way to make him stumble, to warn him that it
would be time to amuse his thoughts with things in the clouds
when he had seen to those at his feet. Indeed she gave him her
good counsel, to look rather to himself than to the sky."

Behavioral finance has spent a great deal of its time contemplating the heavenly vault, at times painfully unaware of the more practical considerations at its feet. My aim here is to provide theory, anecdotes and research sufficient to persuade the mind, but always toward the practical end of making you a better investor.

So read on, but don't just read, because the principles you will learn in this book will only be as useful as your willingness to experiment with them. The journey of the behavioral investor requires a bit of the head, but far more of the heart and stomach.

PART
ONE

The Rules of Behavioral Self-Management

Paradox of Primates & Formalwear

HAVE YOU EVER seen a monkey in a tuxedo? I certainly hope so, but on the off chance that you have not, please put down this book momentarily, access your preferred search engine and see that this travesty is remedied post-haste.

Seen it now? All better then!

In witnessing the transcendent splendor of a monkey in a tuxedo, you probably experienced a number of conflicting responses. Your first response was likely to laugh or smile, but as you looked on, you may have been overcome with a slight unease. For as funny as a monkey in a tuxedo (M.I.A.T., henceforth) may be, there's something not quite right about a wild animal wearing a cummerbund.

As alien as a primate in eveningwear may look, you are at least as out of place when investing in stocks. The sad paradox is this:

1. You must invest in risk assets if you are to survive.
2. You are psychologically ill-equipped to invest in risk assets.

First, let us examine the reasons why you must invest in risk assets if you are to eat anything but cat food in your Golden Years. As of the writing of this book, the median wage in the US is around $49,000.[2]

Let us suppose for illustrative purposes, however, that you are twice as clever as average and have managed to secure a comfortable salary of $100,000 per annum. Let us further suppose you are a disciple of anti-debt guru Dave Ramsey and religiously set aside 10% of your gross income each year into a piggy bank whose innards will not see daylight until the first day of your retirement. Assuming you begin saving at age 25 and retire at age 65, your efforts at self-denial will have yielded a nest egg totaling $400,000.

While $400,000 may seem like a decent sum of money, it hardly provides much for someone who could easily live another 30 years in retirement. At $13,333 per year, you would be living near the poverty line by today's math, to say nothing of how dramatically inflation would have eroded the purchasing power of that figure 40 years on.

If we turn back the clock 45 years from now, we see that roughly $90,000 in 1975 money would get you $400,000 in purchasing power in today's dollars. A little back of the napkin math tells us that even though $400,000 may seem alright today, we will need more like $1.5 million 40 years from now to maintain that same level of purchasing power.

Remember too that the average American couple currently spends nearly $250,000 in retirement on health-related expenses above and beyond their monthly premiums. Factoring in even modest inflation over the next 40 years, the money spent on medical bills alone would far outstrip your savings on the high-earning-always-saving model.

While you could complicate the assumptions above to greater reflect the reality of the average worker (most people don't make $100,000 right out of college, most people get raises over the course of a career, most people don't save 10% of their income), the basic math is the same. You simply aren't going to get to the necessary savings target by age 65 without a little help from risk assets whose returns exceed the insidious and corrosive power of inflation.

As Burton Malkiel said far more succinctly, "It is clear that if we are to cope with even a mild inflation, we must undertake investment strategies that maintain our real purchasing power; otherwise, we are doomed to an ever-decreasing standard of living." So, we must invest if we are to survive.

But, thinking of the second problem raised above, are we any good at investing?

Lewis Carroll's Alice in Wonderland stories are perhaps the best exemplar of the genre known as "literary nonsense." As one might expect from a nonsensical tale, Alice finds herself in a strange world where up is down, wrong is right and "it doesn't much matter which way you go." The book's whimsical circularity is well illustrated in Alice's interactions with the Cheshire Cat, including:

"But I don't want to go among mad people," Alice remarked.

"Oh, you can't help that," said the Cat. "We're all mad here. I'm mad. You're mad."

"How do you know I'm mad?" said Alice.

"You must be," said the Cat, "or you wouldn't have come here."

Much like Alice in the realm of the Cheshire Cat, investors find themselves in a world that defies many of the laws of everyday life. The world of the investor is one in which the future is more certain than the present, doing less work trumps doing more and the collective is less knowledgeable than any single participant. Let us examine each of these realities of this topsy-turvy world in greater detail.

A future more certain than the present?

Suppose I ask you what you will be doing in five minutes. Odds are, you will be able to answer that question with a high degree of certainty. After all, it will probably look a bit like what you are doing at the time you are asked.

Now, let's move the goalposts back a bit and imagine that I ask you what you will be doing five weeks from now. It will certainly be exponentially harder to pinpoint, but your calendar may give some clues as to how you will be engaged at that time. Now imagine you were asked to forecast your actions five months, five years or even 50 years from now. Damn near impossible, right? Of course it is, because in our quotidian existence, the present is far more knowable than the distant future.

What complicates investing is that the exact reverse is true. We have no idea what will happen today, very little notion of what next week holds and a slight inkling as to potential one-year returns. But we could make a much more accurate estimate of 25 years from now. Consider the long-term performance of stocks by holding periods, as shown in table 1.

Table 1—Range of returns on stocks, 1926 to 1997[3]

Holding period (years)	Best return (%)	Worst return (%)
1	+53.9	−43.3
5	+23.9	−12.5
10	+20.1	−0.9
15	+18.2	+0.6
20	+16.9	+3.1
25	+14.7	+5.9

Over short periods of time, returns are nearly unknowable. Over a single year, the range of returns is very wide, from a 54% gain to a 43% loss. Over 25 years, a time period more reflective of a long-term investment horizon, the future becomes far more certain as the range of returns is narrower. Returns vary from a gain of 15% per year to a worst case of around 6% per year for this longer period.

The range of returns is not so scary over the long term, which suggests that stocks ought to be held for the long term. For people, this requires a fundamental rethinking of reality, something that seems not to be happening. As statistician extraordinaire Nate Silver says in *The Signal and the Noise*:

"In the 1950s, the average share of common stock in an American company was held for about six years before being traded— consistent with the idea that stocks are a long-term investment. By the 2000s, the velocity of trading had increased roughly twelvefold. Instead of being held for six years, the same share of stock was traded after just six months. The trend shows few signs of abating: stock market volumes have been doubling once every four or five years."[4]

Intuition tells us that now is more knowable than tomorrow, but Wall Street Bizarro World (WSBW) says otherwise. As Mr. Silver points out, more access to data and the disintermediary effects of technology make our human tendency toward short-termism even greater.

This presents an opportunity for those who can deny this tendency; the growing impatience of the masses only serves to benefit the savvy investor. As Ben Carlson says in *A Wealth of Common Sense*, "Individuals have to understand that no matter what innovations we see in the financial industry, patience will always be the great equalizer in financial markets. There's no way to arbitrage good behavior over a long time horizon. In fact, one of the biggest advantages individuals have over the pros is the ability to be patient."[5]

Do less than you think you should

"Never underestimate the power of doing nothing."
—Winnie the Pooh

"Far from idleness being the root of all evil, it is rather the only true good."
—Søren Kierkegaard

Imagine a world where you could gain more knowledge by reading fewer books, see more of the world by minimizing travel and get more fit by doing less exercise. Certainly, a world where doing less gets you more is highly inconsistent with much of our lived experience, but is just the way Wall Street Bizarro World operates. If we are to learn to live in WSBW (and we must), one of the primary lessons to be learned is to do less than we think we should.

The psychobabble term for the tendency toward dramatic effort in the face of high stakes is *action bias*. Some of the most interesting research into action bias comes to us from the wild world of sports—soccer in particular. A group of researchers examined the behavior of soccer goalies when faced with stopping a penalty kick. By examining 311 kicks, they found that goalies dove dramatically to the right or left side of the goal 94% of the time. The kicks themselves, however, were divided roughly equally, with a third going left, a third right and a third near the middle. This being the case, they found that goalies that stayed in the center of the goal had a 60% chance of stopping the ball; far greater than the odds of going left or right.

So why is it that goalies are given to dramatics when relative laziness is the most sound strategy? The answer becomes more apparent when we put ourselves into the mind of the goalie (especially those who live in countries where failure on the pitch is punishable by death). When the game and national integrity are on the line, you want to look as though you are giving a heroic effort, probabilities be damned! You want to give your all, to "leave it all on the field" in sportspeak, and staying centered has the decided visual impact of stunned complacency. Similarly, investors tasked with preserving and growing their hard-earned wealth do not want to sit idly by in periods of distress, even if the research shows that this is typically the best course of action.

Much like the Guinea worm researchers mentioned in the Introduction, a team at Fidelity set out to examine the behaviors of their best-performing accounts in an effort to isolate the behaviors of truly exceptional investors. What they found may shock you. When they contacted the owners of the best performing accounts, the common thread tended to be that they had forgotten about the account altogether. So much for isolating the complex behavioral traits of skilled investors! It would seem that forgetfulness might be the greatest gift at an investor's disposal.

Another fund behemoth, Vanguard, also examined the performance of accounts that had made no changes versus those who had made tweaks. Sure enough, they found that the "no change" condition handily outperformed the tinkerers. Further, Meir Statman cites research from Sweden showing that the heaviest traders lose 4% of their account value each year to trading costs and poor timing. These results are consistent across the globe: across 19 major stock exchanges, investors who made frequent changes trailed buy and hold investors by 1.5 percentage points per year.[6]

Perhaps the best-known study on the damaging effects of action bias also provides insight into gender-linked tendencies in trading behavior. Terrance Odean and Brad Barber, two of the fathers of behavioral finance, looked at the individual accounts of a large discount broker and found something that surprised them at the time.

The men in the study traded 45% more than the women, with single men out-trading their female counterparts by an incredible 67%. Barber and Odean attributed this greater activity to overconfidence, but whatever its psychological roots, it consistently degraded returns. As a result of overactivity, the average man in the study underperformed the average woman by 1.4 percentage points per year. Worse still, single men lagged single women by 2.3%—an incredible drag when compounded over an investment lifetime.

The tendency of women to outperform is not only seen in retail investors. Female hedge fund managers have consistently and soundly thumped their male colleagues, owing largely to the patience discussed above. As LouAnn Lofton of the *Motley Fool* reports:

"...funds managed by women have, since inception, returned an average 9.06%, compared to just 5.82% averaged by a weighted index of other hedge funds. As if that outperformance weren't impressive enough, the group also found that during the financial panic of 2008, these women-managed funds weren't hurt nearly as severely as the rest of the hedge fund universe, with the funds dropping 9.61% compared to the 19.03% suffered by other funds."[7]

Boys, it would seem, will be hyperactive boys, but few could have guessed the steep financial cost of action bias.

Far from the madding crowd

"Anyone taken as an individual is tolerably sensible and reasonable—as a member of a crowd, he at once becomes a blockhead."

—Friedrich von Schiller

I travel roughly once a week to conferences where, in addition to eating overcooked chicken, I am typically asked to speak to financial advisors about the rudiments of behavioral finance. As anyone who travels for business well knows, it can be tricky in a new city to determine where best to eat, sleep or watch a show. And while many nice hotels provide a concierge to guide you, the concierge's advice is ultimately limited by the fact that it is just one person's opinion.

Having been steered amiss more than once by a concierge with a palate less sophisticated than my own (for surely it could not have been my taste that was in question), I quickly learned to harness the power of the crowdsourced review. Apps like Yelp, Urban Spoon and Rotten Tomatoes provide aggregated reviews that guide diners and moviegoers to restaurants and films that have received consensus acclaim. While I may not always agree with the taste of an individual concierge or my local newspaper's movie reviewer, I have never been disappointed with a movie or dish that has received widespread approval. In things that matter most (i.e., food and movies), there is wisdom in the crowd.

But the power of crowd thinking is not limited to picking out a tasty schnitzel or deciding whether to watch *Dude, Where's My Car?* (18% on Rotten Tomatoes)—it is the bedrock upon which the most successful political systems are built. Sir Winston Churchill famously opined, "The best argument against democracy is a five minute conversation with the average voter", which is a sentiment heard in many forms at election time. So why then has democracy proven to be so successful (or at least not entirely unsuccessful) over long periods of time? Why is it, paraphrasing Churchill again, "the worst form of Government except all those other forms that have been tried from time to time"?

The answer is in the tendency of the crowd to be more wise, ethical, tolerant and gracious than the sum of its parts. The alternatives, political systems like oligarchy and monarchy, live and die with the strengths or weaknesses of the few, which is a much higher risk/reward proposition than democracy. The average voter may be unimpressive, but the average of the averages tends to be the best game in town.

If crowd wisdom can help us solve complex decisional problems and provides us with good-enough government, it seems intuitive that it has something to offer investors, right? Wrong. Once again, the rules of WSBW turn conventional logic on its head and require us to operate from a different set of assumptions. Assumptions that privilege rules-based individual behavior over the wisdom of the crowd.

Why is it that a qualitative gap exists between investment and culinary decisions? Richard Thaler, behavioral economist par excellence, has identified four qualities that make appropriate decision-making in any field difficult. They are:

1. We see the benefits now but the costs later.
2. The decision is made infrequently.
3. The feedback is not immediate.
4. The language is not clear.

Choosing a nice meal consists of clear language ("Our special tonight is deep-fried and smothered in cheese"), immediate feedback ("OMG! This is so good"), is made frequently (three times daily, more if you're like me), and has a mix of immediate and delayed costs ("That will be $27" or "I should have quit after three rolls").

An investment decision on the other hand violates every single one of Thaler's conditions. It consists of intentionally confusing language (What does "market neutral" even mean?), has a massively delayed feedback loop (decades if you're smart), is made very infrequently (thanks for the inheritance, Aunt Mable), and has benefits that are delayed to the point that we can scarcely conceive of them (40-year-old me finds it very hard to imagine the 80-year-old me that will spend this money). The crowd can provide us excellent advice on selecting a meal because it is a decision that is frequently made with results that are instantly known. Conversely, the wisdom or foolishness of a given investment decision may not be made manifest for years, meaning that the impatient crowd may have little wisdom to offer.

As we might expect from Professor Thaler's research, the crowd gets it all wrong deciding when to enter and exit the stock market. They enter at the time of immediate pleasure and long-term pain (bull markets) and leave at the time of immediate pain and long-term pleasure (bear markets). In *A Wealth of Common Sense*, Ben Carlson relates a study performed by the Federal Reserve that examined fund flows from 1984 to 2012. Unsurprisingly, "they found that most investors poured money into the markets after large gains and pulled money out after sustaining losses—a buy high, sell low debacle of a strategy." Yet again we see that preferring the rules of everyday to those of Wall Street Bizarro World means trading cheap emotional comfort for enduring poverty.

Jared Diamond's book *Collapse* recounts the story of a people who tried to do what so many investors attempt in WSBW—inflexibly imposing their preferred way of life on an incompatible system.[8] Diamond tells the story of the Norse, a once powerful group of people who left their homes in Norway and Iceland to settle in Greenland.

The Vikings, who aren't exactly known for their humility, doggedly pushed forward—razing forests, plowing land and building homes— activities that robbed cattle of grazable farmland and depleted the few extant natural resources. Worse still, the Norse ignored the wisdom of the indigenous Inuit people, scorning their ways as primitive compared to what they viewed as a more refined European approach to farming and construction. By ignoring the means by which the native people fed and clothed themselves, the Norse perished in a land of unrecognized plenty, victims of their own arrogance.

Like a Norseman in Greenland, you find yourself of necessity in a land with bizarre customs, some of which make little sense. This land is one in which less is more, the future is more predictable than the present and the wisdom of your peers must be roundly ignored.

It is a lonely place that requires consistency, patience and self-denial, none of which come easily to the human family. But it is a land you must tame if you are to live comfortably and compound your efforts. The laws are few in number and easy enough to learn, but will initially feel uncomfortable in application. It won't be easy but it is surely worth it—and it is all within your power.

Let's move forward now and get to work on learning those laws of the land.

Rule #1
You Control What Matters Most

"The investor's chief problem—and even his worst enemy—is likely to be himself."

—Benjamin Graham

I HAVE REPEATEDLY NOTED that astute observations of human nature are recorded by philosophers, theologians and writers long before science ever proves the underlying truth. One such story is found in the Old Testament and has come to symbolize what I now call River Jordan Problems, or complex problems with simple solutions that go unrecognized precisely because they are so simple.

The story that gives rise to the River Jordan moniker is that of Naaman, a wealthy community leader who is a captain of one of the armies of the King of Syria. By all accounts, Naaman seems to be a powerful man and a respected member of his community. There's just one (big) problem: Naaman is a leper. In an attempt to rid her employer of this most painful encumbrance, one of Naaman's servants suggests that he consult with a holy man in Samaria who is reputed to work miracles for those similarly afflicted.

Having very little to lose, Naaman takes his horse and chariot to the home of Elisha, the holy man, and requests an audience with the prophet. Instead of coming out himself, Elisha sends forth a servant with a simple message for Naaman: "Go and wash in (the River) Jordan seven times, and thy flesh shall come again to thee, and thou shalt be clean."

Now, our powerful protagonist is not happy about this exchange on two counts. First of all, Elisha has not had the common decency to come and speak to him face to face. More egregious still is that he has been told to perform a seemingly inane task in what is a not-so-pretty river (go ahead, Google "River Jordan" and see for yourself how muddy it is). He goes on to name three rivers more beautiful and more proximal before storming off in a rage.

Incensed as he was, Naaman's servants had the courage to approach him and suggest that he follow the simple request of the holy man, saying: "My father, if the prophet had bid thee do some great thing, wouldest thou not have done it? How much rather then, when he saith to thee, Wash, and be clean?" As the story goes, Naaman humbles himself, performs the seemingly simple-minded task and is cleansed of his disease.

Today, investors find themselves beset by a River Jordan Problem that is invisible precisely because of its simplicity. That problem is you.

When considering what drives investment returns, investors are wont to fantasize about everything except the very thing that matters most—their behavior. Some imagine what life would be like if they had bought Tesla (or Apple, or Name-Your-Skyrocketing-Stock) on the day of its initial public offering. Others wonder what it would have been like to perfectly time an exit before the Great Recession. Most common of all, perhaps, is the dream of being a ground floor investor in Berkshire Hathaway, coasting to wealth on the coattails of the folksy guru from the Midwest.

Despite the unequivocal truth that investor behavior is a better predictor of wealth creation than fund selection or market timing, no one dreams about not panicking, making regular contributions and maintaining a long-term focus.

And while it may not be the stuff of investors' dreams, sound behavior is the sine qua non of good investing and principle culprit in ruinous investing. Gary Antonacci uses the DALBAR study of investor behavior to highlight the great chasm between dollar and time weighted returns, the most common shorthand for what we call the "behavior gap":

"Over the past 30 years ending in 2013, the S&P 500 had an annual total return of 11.1%, while the average stock mutual fund investor earned only 3.69%. Around 1.4% of this underperformance was due to mutual fund expenses. Investors making poor timing decisions accounted for much of the remaining 6% of annual underperformance."[9]

The behaviour gap measures the loss that the average investor incurs as a result of emotional responses to market conditions. While some may disagree with DALBAR on methodological grounds, no one doubts that a behavior gap exists. As the estimates in chart 1 show, there is some divergence around the size of the gap—with a range of estimates putting it somewhere between 1.17% and 4.33% per year—but widespread agreement about its return-killing impact.

Chart 1—Estimates of the behavior gap

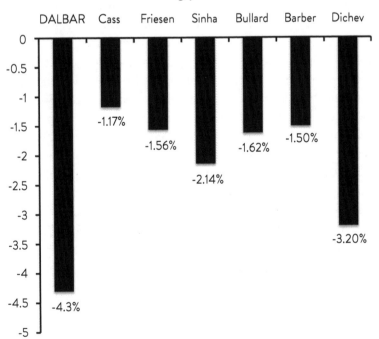

If a mutual fund company created a product that exhibited, say, 4% outperformance year after year, investors would beat down the doors to buy it. Sadly, the River Jordan nature of the behavior gap means that we are much less likely to address the problem when the 4% is earned by virtue of making good decisions.

But OK, let's say you are unmoved by my appeals to minimize the behavior gap and still want to focus on choosing the best funds. Let's concede for a moment that you would be able to do that (despite the fact that there are over 8000 equity mutual funds) and say that you invested in the highest-flying fund of 2000 to 2010.

Over that decade, CGM Focus (CGMFX) was the highest returning stock fund, giving investors 18.2% annualized and besting its nearest rival by over 3% a year. Not bad—way to pick 'em! The only problem is, the average investor in CGMFX lost 10% of her money over the time she was invested. The volatile nature of the fund, paired with the tendency to chase returns, meant that investors piled in after most gains had already been realized, bailed out during times of loss, rinse and repeat. Maximizing returns is a worthwhile pursuit and a focal point of this book, but it is nothing without self-control.

As further evidence of this timing problem, in 1999, at a time when stocks were at their most expensive point in history, Americans were allocating nearly 9% of their paychecks into their 401(k) retirement accounts. Three years later, stocks were about 33% cheaper, but 401(k) contributions had dropped by nearly a quarter.[10] Valuing the broad market is fairly straightforward, but taking the appropriate action based on this valuation is far more difficult.

There is simply no escaping the fact that managing human behavior is the keystone to being a successful investor. No level of investment skill, which is rare on its own, is sufficient to overcome the cancer of bad behavior.

The following nine rules of self-management will point you towards good behavior and help you earn the 4% behavior gap premium, but it can only be accomplished if it is recognized and understood to be within your power. The difficulty with good investment behavior is that even once investors own its importance, what feels natural is seldom the best course of action. The rules of self-management will help combat this as well.

Very few of us have the insight or clarity to manage ourselves in isolation. If good behavior is the best predictor of investment returns, a willingness to seek help is the best predictor of good behavior.

What now?

Think—"Whatever the market does, my own choices matter most."

Ask—"Rather than chasing returns, is there more I could be doing with respect to saving, cutting costs and remaining patient?"

Do—Automate a process of long-term regular contributions to your investment account that escalate with salary raises.

Rule #2
You Cannot Do This Alone

"Non nobis solum nati sumus."

—Marcus Tullius Cicero

I N AN ERA of seven-dollar trades and fee compression, some have been quick to dismiss the traditional advisory relationship as a relic of a bygone era. Years ago, brokers and advisors were the guardians of financial data, the keepers of the stock quote. Today, investors need only an iPhone and a free online brokerage account to do what just 30 years ago was the exclusive purview of Wall Street. It is worth asking in such an age, "Is my advisor really earning her fee?" An appeal to the research shows that the answer is a resounding "yes", albeit not for the reasons you might have supposed.

In a seminal paper titled 'Advisor's Alpha', the famously fee-sensitive folks at Vanguard estimated that the value added by working with a competent financial advisor is roughly 3% per year.[11] The paper is quick to point out that the 3% delta will not be achieved in a smooth, linear fashion. Rather, the benefits of working with an advisor will be "lumpy" and most concentrated during times of profound fear and greed. This uneven distribution of advisor value presages a second truth that we will discuss shortly; the best use of a financial advisor is as a behavioral coach rather than an asset manager.

Further evidence of advisor efficacy is added by Morningstar in their white paper, 'Alpha, Beta, and Now... Gamma'.[12] "Gamma" is

Morningstar's shorthand for "the extra income an investor can earn by making better financial decisions" and they cast improving decision-making as the primary benefit of working with a financial advisor. In their attempt at quantifying Gamma, Morningstar arrived at a figure of 1.82% per year outperformance for those receiving advice aimed at improving their financial choices. Again, it would seem that advisors are more than earning their fee and that improving decision-making is the primary means by which they improve clients' investment outcomes.

Research conducted by Aon Hewitt and managed accounts provider Financial Engines also supports the idea that help pays big dividends. Their initial research was conducted from 2006 to 2008 and compared those receiving help in the form of online advice, guidance through target date funds or managed accounts to those who did it themselves. Their finding during this time was that those who received help outperformed those who did not by 1.86% per annum, net of fees.

Seeking to examine the impact of help during times of volatility, they subsequently performed a similar analysis of help versus no-help groups that included the uncertain days of 2009 and 2010. They found the impact of decision-making assistance was heightened during times of volatility and the outperformance of the group receiving assistance grew to 2.92% annually, net of fees.

Just as was suggested by Vanguard from the outset, the benefits of advice are disproportionately experienced during times when rational decision-making becomes most difficult.

We have now established that financial guidance tends to pay off somewhere in the ballpark of 2% to 3% a year. Although those numbers may seem small at first blush, anyone familiar with the marvel of compounding understands the enormous power of such outperformance. If financial advice really does work, the effect of following good advice over time should be substantial. Indeed, the research suggests that very thing.

In their 2012 'Value of Advice Report' the Investment Funds Institute of Canada found that investors who purchase financial advice are more than one and a half times more likely to stick with their long-term investment plan than those who do not. Because of this commitment to a game plan, the wealth discrepancies between families that receive advice and those who do not grow over time. For those who receive four to six years of advice, the multiple attributable to advice is 1.58. Those receiving 7 to 14 years of advice nearly double up (1.99x) their no-advice peers and those receiving 15 or more years of advice clocked in at an overwhelming 2.73x multiple. Good financial advice pays in the short run, but the multiplication of those gains over an investing lifetime is truly staggering.

Hopefully at this point there is little doubt in your mind that the cumulative effects of receiving sound investment counsel are financially impressive. But as we look beyond dollars and cents, it is worth considering whether there are quality of life benefits to be enjoyed by working with a financial professional.

After all, many people perfectly capable of mowing a lawn, cleaning a home or painting a room hire those jobs out. While you may have lawn mowing skill equal to that of the person you hire, you may still enjoy peace of mind and increased time with loved ones as a result of your delegation. The research suggests that in addition to the financial rewards that may accrue to those working with an advisor, it also provides increases in confidence and security that are no less valuable.

The Canadian 'Value of Advice Report' found that those paying for financial advice reported a greater sense of confidence, and more certainty about their ability to retire comfortably and having higher levels of funds for an emergency. A separate study performed by the Financial Planning Standards Council found that 61% of those paying for financial advice answered affirmatively to, "I have peace of mind" compared to only 36% of their "no plan" peers. The majority (54%) of those with a plan felt prepared in the event of an emergency, versus only 22% of those without a plan. Finally, 51% of respondents with a plan felt prepared for retirement against a frightening 18% of those not receiving advice.[13]

Receiving good financial advice pays a dividend that builds both wealth and confidence. The research is unequivocal that a competent financial guide can help you achieve the returns necessary to arrive at your financial destination while simultaneously improving the quality of your journey.

Ten questions for your financial advisor

We've established that working with a financial advisor can help save you from yourself. But not all advisors are created equal. Ask the following ten questions of a potential advisor to ensure that you are working with the best.

1. **Are you a fiduciary?** A fiduciary has a legal requirement to place his clients' interest ahead of his own.
2. **How will you keep me from being my own worst enemy?** Don't forget, behavioral coaching is an advisor's greatest added value!
3. **How do you charge and how much?** Fees are more negotiable than you might imagine, especially for larger accounts.
4. **Do you have a niche?** Some advisors specialize in working with small business owners, "women in transition" or those with values-based investment preferences.
5. **What services do you offer?** Some financial professionals offer only planning or investment advice, while others offer a broad range of services. Ensure that what is offered is consistent with your needs.
6. **What are your credentials?** Look for some combination of years of experience, appropriate certifications and post-graduate education.
7. **What is your investment philosophy?** A clear and concise investment philosophy is a sign of having given this deep thought. A corny sales pitch is a sign that you should run.
8. **How often will we communicate?** This should be driven by your needs and preferences. Expect between one and four times per year.
9. **What is unique about your client experience?** You are paying good money for this service and should be treated accordingly.
10. **What is your succession plan?** Someone asking you to think about the long term should have done so as well.

Value where you least expect it

We began the last chapter with a brief explanation of River Jordan Problems, or problems with parsimonious solutions that are often ignored because of their simplicity. Naaman scoffed at the suggestion of the holy man, precisely because the answer seemed inelegant next to the hugeness and complexity of his problem. Similarly, we now tend to look for complex (e.g., medicinal) remedies for most physical ailments while ignoring powerful but simple behavioral interventions like improving diet, increasing exercise and engaging in quiet reflection.

This tendency to seek complexity and ignore simplicity has been alive and well for years in investment circles and has led advisors and clients alike to ignore the greatest value added by a financial professional. Once again, we will appeal to the research to try and determine the sources of outperformance for those receiving professional financial advice.

Vanguard's 'Advisor's Alpha' study did an excellent job of quantifying the value added (in basis points, or bps) by many of the common activities performed by an advisor, and the results may surprise you. They include:

- Rebalancing—35 bps
- Asset allocation—0 to 75 bps
- Behavioral coaching—150 bps

Interestingly, behavioral coaching (read hand-holding) provides more added value than any of the activities more directly associated with the management of money. Based on Vanguard's assumption of 3% per year average added value, fully half of that owes to behavioral coaching, or preventing clients from making foolish decisions during times of fear or greed! Put more plainly still, an advisor is adding more value when she is managing your emotions than when she is managing your money.

Morningstar's 'Gamma' study is also illustrative of the true value added by an advisor and the things investors should seek out when choosing a professional. It lists the sources of added values as follows:

- Asset allocation
- Withdrawal strategy
- Tax efficiency
- Product allocation
- Goals-based advice

While some sources of gamma can easily be self-taught (e.g., asset allocation), others remain uniquely powerful in the hands of an outside advisor. Just as anyone can look up a sensible workout regimen, it is not difficult to find instructions on investing in a broadly diversified mix of asset classes.

But if knowledge were sufficient to induce appropriate behavior, America would not now be the most obese developed country in the world and staring down the barrel of a looming retirement crisis. While appropriate knowledge is an important starting point, a personal coach that ensures adherence to a plan is demonstrably even more important.

So, do financial advisors add value?

The research strongly supports that they do, both in terms of improving means and quality of life. But they only add value when we know what to look for when selecting the appropriate wealth management partner. Our natural tendencies will be toward excess complexity and flashy marketing, seeking out those who lead with bold claims of esoteric knowledge. What will add much greater richness is a partner who balances deep knowledge with deep rapport. Someone we will listen to when we are scared and who will save us from ourselves. A simple solution to a complex problem; I think Naaman would approve.

What now?

Think—"An advisor who keeps me from making five big mistakes over a lifetime has more than earned her money."

Ask—"If an advisor's primary value is coaching my behavior, what might I look for in a potential advisor relationship?"

Do—Enlist the help of an advisor who sees behavioral coaching as one of her primary responsibilities.

Rule #3
Trouble Is Opportunity

*"The time of maximum pessimism is the best time to buy,
and the time of maximum optimism is the best time to sell."*

—**Sir John Templeton**

YOU LIKELY KNOW that Nietzsche famously quipped, "That which
does not kill us makes us stronger." What you may not have
known is that he said this immediately before contracting syphilis,
having a mental breakdown and dying of an unpleasant combination
of psychosis, strokes and paralysis.[14]

In life as in financial markets, it is easy to talk a good game about
being greedy when others are fearful, but it is quite another thing to do
it. A great deal of this difficulty owes to the particular ways in which
we are wired to process and hold on to negative events.

Let's assume for the sake of a quick thought experiment that you are
having a good-if-somewhat-unspectacular day. I want you to take 30
to 60 seconds to imagine what could make this day significantly better
and write it down. Now I'd like you to consider what could make
this day much worse. Please take 30 to 60 seconds and create a list of
what could really ruin this day. Now take a moment to compare the
two lists—which list is longer? Which list is more vivid? Which list is
more realistic?

If you're like most people, it was much easier for you to generate
a list of catastrophic events than it was to come up with things that

could really make your day. We have a natural tendency to imagine the worst and remember negative events, as a sort of protection against future harm. This tendency to catastrophize is well understood by people selling all sorts of things, the financial press chief among them. As Nick Murray says, "There is virtually always an apocalypse du jour going on somewhere in the world. And on the rare occasions when there is not, journalism will simply invent one, and present it 24/7 as the incipient end of the world."

There are three things that intelligent investors must understand if they are to truly inoculate themselves against the fear peddled by the profiteers of peril: corrections and bear markets are a common part of any investment lifetime, they represent a long-term buying opportunity and a systematic process is required to take advantage of them.

A "correction" is defined as a 10% drop in stock prices, whereas a "bear market" is defined as a 20% drop. Both definitions are entirely arbitrary, but inasmuch as they are widely watched and impact the behaviour of other investors, they are worth considering.

From 1900 to 2013, the US stock market experienced 123 corrections—an average of one per year! The more dramatic losses that are the hallmark of a bear market occur slightly less frequently, averaging one every 3.5 years. Although the media talks about 10% to 20% market losses as though they are the end of the world, they arrive as regularly as spring flowers and have not negated the tendency of markets to dramatically compound wealth over long periods of time.

It is incredible to consider that over that 100 plus years, one could expect both double digit annualized returns with attendant double digit percentage losses. This being the case, please repeat after me: "Bear markets are a natural part of the economic cycle and I should expect 10 to 12 in my lifetime."

Table 2 provides the dates of US bear markets since 1929, their duration in months and the extent of their peak to trough declines.

Bear markets and corrections arrive with some regularity and force, but their power to destroy returns is as much behavioral as it is financial. Carl Richards, author of *The Behavior Gap*, gives the example of October 2002, "the fifth month in a row that investors pulled more money out of stock mutual funds than they put into them—the first time ever such a streak had occurred." Care to guess the bottom of that bear market from which stocks nearly doubled over the next five years? Yep—October 2002.

This tendency to misbehave is not limited to retail investors by any means. As Burton Malkiel shares in *A Random Walk Down Wall Street*:

"Caution on the part of mutual fund managers (as represented by a very high cash allocation) coincides almost perfectly with troughs in the stock market. Peaks in mutual funds' cash positions have coincided with market troughs during 1970, 1974, 1982, and the end of 1987 after the great stock-market crash."

Table 2—US bear markets since 1929

Correction	Events	Market peak	Peak to trough (%)	Duration (months)
Crash of 1929	Excessive leverage; irrational exuberance	Sep 1929	−86	33
1937 Fed Tightening	Premature policy tightening	Mar 1937	−60	63
Post WWII Crash	Post-war demobilization; recession fears	May 1946	−30	37
Flash Crash of 1962	Flash crash; Cuban Missile Crisis	Dec 1961	−28	7
Tech Crash of 1970	Economic overheating; civil unrest	Nov 1968	−36	18
Stagflation	OPEC oil embargo	Jan 1973	−48	21
Volcker Tightening	Targeting inflation	Nov 1980	−27	21
1987 Crash	Program trading; overheating markets	Aug 1987	−34	3
Tech Bubble	Extreme valuations; dotcom boom-bust	Mar 2000	−49	31
Global Financial Crisis	Leverage/housing; Lehman collapse	Oct 2007	−57	17
Average			−45	25

The wealth-destroying impacts of bear markets are greatly magnified by our reactions to fear. This is made doubly hard by the fact that our subjective experience of the markets is exactly the reverse of what it ought to be; the market feels most scary when it is actually most safe. As Warren Buffett's mentor said, "The investor who permits himself to be stampeded or unduly worried by unjustified market declines in his holdings is perversely transforming his basic advantage into a basic disadvantage."[15] The only hope for managing this undue worry is a systematic approach to investing and the will to see it through—much more on that later.

The average adult spends about one of every eight hours contemplating the future. That means that on average, you spend two of your waking hours each day wondering what tomorrow will bring. Unfortunately, since worry tends to be stickier (remember that catastrophic day you dreamed up?) than peace of mind, the preponderance of that two hours is spent wondering if tomorrow will be okay. All of this worry fails to realize that times of market turmoil tend to presage periods of great returns.

Take for instance the counterintuitive truth that periods of high unemployment have tended to lead to stock market outperformance.[16] Consider too Ben Carlson's finding that, "Markets don't usually perform the best when they go from good to great. They actually show the best performance when things go from terrible to not-quite-so-terrible as before." *The Elements of Investing* by Burton Malkiel and Charlie Ellis has a quote about the approach of standing firm through the market's ups and downs that should resonate with parents (and former teenagers) everywhere: "Investing is like raising teenagers—'interesting' along the way as they grow into fine adults. Experienced parents know to focus on the long-term, not the dramatic daily dustups."

Have you ever wondered why you can't tickle your own arm? The reason is that your brain has to have the thought, "Hey, I ought to tickle myself" before you can engage in that act. By the time you actually do attempt to tickle your arm, your body sees it coming and the effect is far more muted than if your partner were to tickle that same arm.

Forming reasonable assumptions about market volatility has a similar impact—expectation dulls the impact. If you buy the media hype that the sky is falling, you will be cut by the two-edged sword of financial and behavioral loss. However, if you are able to view corrections as natural at worst and opportunities at best, you will be positioned to profit from others' panic.

What now?

Think—"Bear markets, recessions and especially uncertainty are the psychological price I pay for strong returns."

Ask—"Do the events causing others to panic provide opportunities for me?"

Do—Create a list of high-quality-but-overpriced dream stocks to buy when market volatility makes prices more attractive.

Rule #4

If You're Excited, It's A Bad Idea

"If investing is entertaining, if you're having fun, you're probably not making any money. Good investing is boring."

—George Soros

WHEN GIVING SEMINARS on risk assessment, I often ask participants to write down the word that if spelled phonetically would be "dahy." Please take a second to write it down yourself and don't over think it.

There are obviously two ways to spell that sound in English: "dye" or "die." The word that first popped into your head may have everything to do with the sort of mood you are in. Since mood colors memory retrieval, those having a good day are more likely to think of the less treacherous spelling, while those having a tough day may have mortality on the brain.

But the effects of mood on thinking are not limited to simple retrieval. Emotion also impacts the way we remember the past and think about the future. Ask someone having a bad day (those that wrote "die," I'm looking at you) about their childhood and they are likely to tell you how they were chubby, had pimples and never got picked first for kickball. Ask that same person on a sunnier day and they may recall summers in Nantucket and triple dips from the Tastee Freeze.

We often analogize our brains to computers—impartial storage apparatus tasked with housing and calling up information objectively. In reality, our brains are far more like beer goggles than supercomputers, which means that the intelligent investor must take precautions to ensure the emotion of the moment is not warping his sense of reality. Institutional investor Ben Carlson puts it very bluntly: "There are many areas in your life that call for emotional reactions—you should get emotional on your wedding day or during the birth of your child. But emotions are the enemy of good investment decisions. Let me repeat that one more time for effect: emotions are the enemy of good investment decisions."[17]

A study conducted by social psychologist Jennifer Lerner and her colleagues helps put some numbers to the idea that emotion can impact our assessment of risk and our willingness to pay.[18] Lerner and her team divided study participants into two groups—Sadness and No Emotion. Those in the Sadness group watched a clip from the movie *The Champ*, in which a young boy's mentor dies. They were then asked to further empathize with this loss by writing a paragraph talking about how this death would have impacted them emotionally. Those in the No Emotion group watched a short clip about fish and were asked to write about day-to-day activities. After watching these clips, participants were told that they were now undertaking a second, unrelated study. In this study, some of the participants were asked to set a price at which they would sell a highlighter pen and others were asked to suggest a price at which they would buy the pen.

The results of the study support what we might now expect—emotion had an enormous impact on the price at which buying and selling took place. Buyers in the Sadness condition were willing to pay around 30% more for the highlighter than those in the No Emotion condition. Their sadness led them to overpay in just the way that retail therapy purchases may seem frivolous after the fact. Sellers in the Sadness condition also showed the scars of emotion—selling their pens for around 33% less than their No Emotion peers.

Very little is on the line when discussing overpaying for a pen, but if we extrapolate this to our personal wealth the effects would be quite dramatic. An emotional investor is one who would overpay for shares given her excitement and part with shares too cheaply in despair. It would appear that financial writer Walter Bagehot was on to something, long before the advent of behavioral finance, when he wrote, "All people are most credulous when they are most happy."[19]

Under the influence

Furthering our look at the way that mood impacts risk perception, let's now turn to the work of the affable behavioral economist Dan Ariely. In *Predictably Irrational*, Ariely reports on some—um, stimulating—work done by himself and a group of colleagues. Ariely and company asked a group of students 19 questions about their sexual preferences, including their propensity to engage in "odd" sexual behaviors, cheat on a partner, practice safe sex and engage respectfully with their partner.

They first asked these questions of the students in a "cold" state in which they were emotionally and sexually unaroused. As you might have guessed, the tendency among the students in the cold state was to advocate safe, consensual sex that respected the wishes of the partner and occurred within the context of an existing relationship.

Next, Ariely and team introduced emotion into the exercise in the form of pornographic images aimed at sexually and emotionally arousing the participants. When sexually aroused, the answers of the participants to the 19 questions changed dramatically. They were 136% more likely to cheat on a partner, 72% more likely to engage in odd sexual activities and 25% more likely to have unprotected sex. Ariely sums it up thusly, "Prevention, protection, conservatism, and morality disappeared completely from the radar screen. They were simply unable to predict the degree to which passion would change them."[20]

The lurid nature of the experiment may lead us to believe that its impact is limited to sexual arousal, but that would be a mistake. As Ariely says in a footnote, "...we can also assume that other emotional states (anger, hunger, excitement, jealousy, and so on) work in similar ways, making us strangers to ourselves."[21]

The students in the study knew all of the rules—you always wear a condom and you never cheat on your partner—they just didn't care about the rules in the heat of the moment. So too are you aware of many of the rules of smart investing—they just seem obsolete in a moment of fear or greed. Psychologist and trading coach Brett Steenbarger says it well, "...the net effect of emotion on trading appears to be a disruption of rule governance... Under emotional conditions, however, their [traders'] attention became self-focused to the point where they were no longer attentive to their rules. Often, it wasn't so much a case that under emotional conditions they doubted their rules; rather, they simply forgot them."[22] No matter how smart, an emotional investor is a stranger to himself and his rules.

Ten quick tips for managing emotion

Emotion impacts our perception of everything, including time, risk and appropriate price. Here are some practical suggestions for keeping emotion in check:

1. Exercise vigorously
2. Redefine the problem
3. Limit intake of caffeine and alcohol
4. Talk to a friend
5. Don't react right away
6. Shift the focus of your attention
7. Label your emotions
8. Write down your thoughts and feelings
9. Challenge catastrophic thoughts
10. Control whatever aspects possible

Story time

There are many reasons to be excited about a stock. It may be a company or product that you personally use, you may have overheard a friend recommending the shares at a cocktail party, or perhaps you want to be an early investor in the next big thing. Whatever the cause of your excitement, it is likely that it is packaged in some broader narrative, the conclusion of which is, "…she became exceedingly wealthy and lived happily ever after." Stories bypass reason, skip the brain and head straight for the heart. For this reason, stories are also the enemy of the behavioral investor.

Consider how much you would pay for a single, sequined glove, in a dated 1980s fashion. Not much, I'd wager. Now, how much would you pay if I told you that the glove had been worn by Michael Jackson? The story would completely change the means by which you value the item. This is not so dangerous with 1980s pop paraphernalia, but very dangerous when buying stocks.

Writers Rob Walker and Joshua Glenn understood the power of narrative and created a sort of social experiment that they called The Significant Objects Project. It was designed to test their assumption that "narrative transforms the insignificant into the significant." Walker and Glenn purchased 100 items of garage sale quality and had their writer friends trump them up with fictional backstories. All told, the junky items cost just under $130, but they were able to sell them for over $3600 on eBay. Yes, the power of story led eBay users to pay $52 for a used oven mitt.

Nowhere is the power of narrative more fully realized than in IPO (initial public offering) investing. IPOs are definitionally novel, often focused in new and growing sectors, and companies tend to go public at times of great bullishness. The power of narrative, emotion and fear of missing out combine to make IPOs extremely appealing to both professional and retail investors. So how has all of this excitement served the investing public? Cogliati, Paleari and Vismara show in 'IPO Pricing: Growth Rates Implied in Offer Prices' that the average IPO in the US has gone on to underperform the market benchmark by 21% per year in the first three years following its release.[23] Despite this massive underperformance, there is no good reason to suppose that the demand for IPOs will wane in popularity in the years to come. After all, there will always be stories.

The ills wrought by emotional investing are legion, but perhaps the primary damage done is by way of truncating our time horizon. Long-term commitment to a plan is the purview of a cool head, but emotion says, "I want it now." Four Princeton psychologists demonstrated this conclusively by conducting brain scans of participants who were given two options: a $15 Amazon gift card now or a $20 Amazon gift card in two weeks. The study showed that:

> "...the possibility of getting that $15 gift certificate *now!* caused an unusual flurry of stimulation in the limbic areas of most students' brains—a whole grouping of brain structures that's primarily responsible for our emotional life, as well as the formation of memory. The more the students were emotionally excited about something, the psychologists found, the greater the chances of their opting for the immediate, if less immediately gratifying, alternatives."[24]

Indeed, an excited investor is an impatient investor and an impatient investor is a broke investor.

In most areas of life, emotion serves an important role and should be given careful consideration. Emotion helps us empathize with our loved ones, moves us to do good in the world and can lead to some of life's richest moments. That it should be so fully expunged from investment decision-making is yet another example of the vast chasm between Real Life and Wall Street Bizarro World. So, laugh, cry, love and get angry—just not here.

What now?

Think—"Emotion makes me a stranger to common sense."
Ask—"Is this decision animated by fear or greed?"
Do—Keep a small investment account (maybe around 3% of your total wealth) separate from your long-term investments to allow for experimentation and tinkering.

Rule #5
You Are Not Special

"You are not special. You are not a beautiful or unique snowflake. You are the same decaying organic matter as everything else."

—**Chuck Palahniuk,** *Fight Club*

"I do not like to work with patients who are in love. Perhaps it is because of envy—I too crave enchantment. Perhaps it is because love and psychotherapy are fundamentally incompatible. The good therapist fights darkness and seeks illumination, while romantic love is sustained by mystery and crumbles upon inspection. I hate to be love's executioner."

So says Dr. Irvin Yalom, Stanford professor and the author of, in this shrink's humble estimation, some of the finest books on psychology produced in the last 50 years. While Yalom's pronouncements here deal most directly with romantic love in a therapeutic setting, their application to capital markets is obvious to me. Just as good therapy is about seeking personal illumination, good investing is about overcoming the belief in personal uniqueness that leads us to overlook probability-based approaches in favor of a vague belief that, "The rules don't apply to me."

Investors who own their mediocrity are able to rely on rules and systems—they do what works and reap the rewards. Investors mired in a need to be better than average insist on flaunting the rules in favor of their own ideas and pay a steep price for their arrogance. Just as Yalom was "love's executioner" to catalyze true introspection in his clients, you must ruthlessly execute your own ego to achieve exceptional investment results. As investor and author James P. O'Shaughnessy says, "The key to successful investing is to recognize that we are just as susceptible to crippling behavioral biases as the next person."[25]

Our tendency toward pride is rooted in a handful of well-documented cognitive errors, including a belief in our personal exceptionality known as overconfidence bias, and the tendency to own success and delegate misfortune, known as the fundamental attribution error. James Montier reports that over 95% of people think they have a better than average sense of humor.[26] Peters and Waterman, in their book In Search of Excellence, found that 100% of men surveyed thought they were better than average interpersonally and that 94% of men felt as though they were athletically better than average.[27]

When worldwide mathematical proficiency is considered, American high school students are squarely middle of the pack. However, when these same students are asked about how confident they are in their abilities, they lead the world. As CNBC's Josh Brown noted of this study, "While there is probably something to be said for self-confidence in general, the combination of mathematical mediocrity paired with overconfidence is a lot of what's wrong with the investment world today."[28] A belief in personal exceptionality causes us to ignore potential danger, take excessively concentrated stock positions and stray from areas of personal competence. It is typical of Wall Street Bizarro World that an admission of our own mediocrity is what is required for investment excellence.

If the scope of the problem were limited to men's faulty assumptions about their physiques it might not be so damaging, but dangerous overconfidence is apparent among both novice and professional investors as well. Meir Statman writes in *What Investors Really Want*:

"At the height of the stock market in February 2000, individual investors surveyed by Gallup expected, on average, that the stock market would deliver a 13.3% return during the following 12 months. But, on average, they expected their own portfolios to deliver 15.5 percent... Members of the American Association of

Individual Investors overestimated their own investment returns by an average of 3.4 percentage points relative to their actual returns, and they overestimated their own returns relative to those of the average investor by 5.1 percentage points."

As Statman suggests, investor overconfidence exists on an absolute and relative basis. Remember that in early 2000, stocks were the most expensive they have ever been in the history of the US stock market by any reasonable measure. To hope for returns 1.5 times the historical average from a place of already astronomical valuations is the definition of overconfidence. Expecting to beat all of your peers in the process is the cherry on top.

Montier's fundamental attribution error, cited above, is the effect that makes us quick to integrate contextual cues into our appraisals of ourselves but slow to give others the same nuanced appraisal. Instead, we see their failings as more absolute and organic. On your morning commute, this looks like you screaming at others to "Watch where you are going!" even as you ascribe your own bad driving to not yet having had your second cup of coffee. When you are unkind to someone, you chalk it up to having a bad day. When someone is unkind to you, they are rotten at their core—it is who they are.

This tendency to own success and outsource failure leads us to view all investment successes as personal skill, thereby robbing us of opportunities for learning as well as any sense of history. When your stocks go up, you credit your personal genius. When your stocks go down, you fault externalities. Meanwhile, you learn nothing. When legendary investor Jeremy Grantham was asked what he thought investors would learn from the Great Recession he responded, "In the short term, a lot. In the medium term, a little. In the long term, nothing at all. That is the historical precedent."[29] Arrogance is the enemy of the very self-reflection that saves us from ourselves and allows us to learn from history.

Underweighting the downside

Warren Buffett's first rule of investing is "Don't lose money" and his second rule is "Never forget the first rule." Wise investors throughout time have understood the simple truth that, while offense makes the headlines, defense wins championships. The great danger of the fundamental attribution error then is not that it makes us arrogant about our desired upside, it's that it makes us careless about the downside. A belief in personal exceptionalism leads us to underweight negative probabilities; a sure recipe for disaster in investment decision-making.

Cook College performed a study in which people were asked to rate the likelihood that a number of positive events (e.g., win the lottery, marry for life) and negative events (e.g., die of cancer, get divorced) would impact their lives. What they found was hardly surprising—participants overestimated the likelihood of positive events by 15% and underestimated the probability of negative events by 20%. Likewise, Heather Lench and Peter Ditto performed a study where participants were shown six positive and six negative life events as well as their accompanying probability in the general population. Respondents endorsed 4.75 of the 6 positive life events as probably impacting them but only 2.4 of the negative life events, roundly ignoring the actual probabilities altogether.

What this tells us is that we tend to personalize the positive and delegate the dangerous. I might win the lottery, she might die of cancer. We might live happily ever after, they might get divorced. Other people might need to follow the rules when selecting a stock, but I just have a gut feel. We understand that bad things happen, but in service of living a happy life, we tend to think about those things in the abstract.

The risk management implications of perceived uniqueness are obvious—if we make decisions with the mindset that we are a unique snowflake, we are likely to ignore potential risks. Simply put, if upside potential is "all me" and losing money is the birthright of those other schmucks, we are bound to do stupid things. As always, someone else (J. K. Galbraith) has said it far better than I ever could: "Fools, as it has long been said, are indeed separated, soon or eventually, from their money. So, alas, are those who, responding to a general mood of optimism, are captured by a sense of their own financial acumen. Thus it has been for centuries; thus in the long future it will also be."[30]

In ancient Rome, victorious military leaders were paraded through the streets to be celebrated by the masses, much as today we celebrate the rock star investment managers at conferences and on the sets of 24-hour business networks. But there is one edge the Roman victors held over the modern day Wall Street warrior—a behavioral intervention meant to overcome the damning effects of hubris and recency bias. Behind the general, in the same chariot, was placed a slave whose sole responsibility was to remind the general of his mortality as a hedge against excessive pride, the kind that comes before the fall. "Memento mori," the slave would whisper, "Someday you will die." Even on the general's greatest day, the Romans included a mechanism by which the conqueror was reminded that he would be on the receiving end of bad luck at some future date.

It is natural to want to applaud our financial successes and take some credit. But even as we celebrate, we would be wise to do as the Romans and ground ourselves in the sobering reality of our imperfection and impermanence. "Respice post te! Hominem te esse memento!" the slaves would further say, "Look behind you and remember that you are a man."

What now?

Think—"I am no wiser or more self-controlled than other market participants."

Ask—"Why have others passed on this if it is such a great investment opportunity?"

Do—Follow the guidance of your advisor and your written financial plan rather than a notion of personal superiority.

Rule #6

Your Life Is The Best Benchmark

"A wealthy man is one who earns $100 more than his wife's sister's husband."

—H. L. Mencken

Mirror, mirror

Yawn.

YAWN.

Yaaaaaawwwwwwn.

Are you yawning after reading this? I'm fighting back the urge myself after writing the word three times. What gives? The answer to this extreme suggestibility lies with what scientists call mirror neurons—neurons that fire both when an action is being performed and when that same action is being observed.[31]

The original discovery of mirror neurons took place in a sleepy, somewhat overlooked research lab in Parma, Italy. Scientists there were studying the brains of macaque monkeys in an effort to understand how the brain organizes motor behavior. As Martin Lindstrom explains, the scientists very quickly discovered some things that challenged their assumptions about how the brain works. "They observed that the macaques' premotor neurons would light up not just when the monkeys reached for that nut, but also when they saw other monkeys reaching for a nut." Whether an action was performed by the monkey or merely observed, the effect on the brain was identical.

Stranger still was what they observed one sweltering afternoon when one of the graduate students on the team entered the lab with an ice cream cone. One of the monkeys, still hooked up to the monitoring apparatus, was staring greedily at the frosty treat. As the grad student brought the ice cream closer for a lick, the macaque's premotor region began lighting up the screen. "It hadn't moved its arm or taken a lick of ice cream; it wasn't even holding anything at all. But simply by observing the student bringing the ice cream cone to his mouth, the monkey's brain had mentally imitated the very same gesture."[32]

Party of one

Mirror neurons are the reason why you cry at a sad movie, cringe at the sight of someone else eating something gross, or close your eyes when the chainsaw-wielding hillbilly stumbles upon the unsuspecting group of college kids at the lake house. Mirror neurons are why "unboxing" videos exist. It's nearly as fun to watch someone else open a new gaming system or expensive toy as it is to do it ourselves. To truly apply this learning, give your kids a video of other children opening presents at their next birthday party and tell them Dr. Crosby told you it's more or less the same thing!

The power of social mimicry can certainly work for good—we might cry with a friend who has lost a parent we never met—but can it also be used to manipulate our behavior? Consider the dreaded laugh track. I bet if we were to take a poll of the thousands of people who will read this book, exactly zero of them would endorse the statement, "I like sitcom laugh tracks." Laugh tracks are corny, obnoxious and obtrusive, and the laughter itself often sounds inauthentic.

If laugh tracks are so universally disliked, why do Hollywood executives continue to include them? These executives understand something that we may not; however irksome canned laughter may be, it provides valuable social cues to viewers. Research has repeatedly shown that laugh tracks cause viewers to laugh longer and harder and to rate the viewing experience as more enjoyable.[33] In fact, laugh tracks have been shown to be most effective at improving the appraisals of jokes that are especially bad! We are programmed to do what others are doing, even when those others only exist on tape.

Social mimicry is ubiquitous. Panhandlers often salt their tip jars with money from the day before to show that giving is proper behavior and that other people have deemed them worthy of a handout. A beggar with no money in his cup is perhaps more deserving of a dollar, but also far less likely to get that dollar than the beggar who already has three.

One of the most cost effective ways to extinguish a fear in children is to have them observe other children performing the anxiety-inducing behavior. In one study, 67% of children with a fear of dogs were "cured" of this phobia within a week, simply by watching other children pet Fido.[34] Even something as serious as suicide is subject to the effects of social mimicry. Dr. David Phillips of the University of California at San Diego found that "within two months after every front-page suicide story, an average of fifty-eight more people than usual killed themselves."[35] In laughing and crying, living and dying, it would seem that the behavior of those around is far more contagious than we may have ever supposed.

Mirror neurons and other mechanisms of the brain facilitate the precious gift of empathy, an invaluable resource when building relationships and community. Though we may not have experienced exactly the same joys and sorrows, we can vicariously experience each other's emotions in a way that allows for comfort, support and even shared elation.

But, in what is becoming an ever-stronger theme here, the very mechanisms by which we form community and share each others' burdens make us poor investors and more concerned with keeping up with others than providing for our own needs. As Jason Zweig says, "…investing isn't about beating others at their game. It's about controlling yourself at your own game."[36]

Keeping score

It is natural in most any human endeavor to set a benchmark against which we gauge performance. After all, an athletic contest without a scoreboard may be good recreation but it would be awfully boring viewing. However, as surely as we need a scoreboard, we must ensure that we are keeping score in a manner that is personally meaningful and consistent with the rules of the game.

For most investors, keeping score means falling prey to the Procrustean fallacy of comparing their returns to those of the equity market benchmark—typically the S&P 500. In Greek mythology, Procrustes was an innkeeper with just one size of bed. In order to ensure goodness of fit between his travelers and his accommodations, he would cut the limbs off of travelers that were too large for his bed and stretch the bodies of more diminutive guests. So too do investors torture and contort their risk preferences, personal values and return expectations when benchmarking to an impersonal market index rather than something more customized to their needs.

In addition to the intuitive appeal of measuring your own performance against your own needs, it also has a host of psychological benefits that make us better investors. Measuring performance against personal needs rather than an index has been shown to keep us invested during periods of market volatility, enhance savings behavior and help us maintain a long-term focus.

The industry term for benchmarking to personal needs is goals-based-investing. Although each asset management firm has its own approach, the broad commonalities are that individual return needs are decided upon and investments are bucketed into several tranches that correspond with personal goals. SEI Investments was one of the first firms to roll out a goals-based platform and had the good fortune (at least for researchers like myself) of doing so right before the financial crisis of 2008. This auspicious timing allows us to observe the behavioral impact of a goals-based approach to wealth management versus the more traditional approach of comparing returns to the broader market. As I wrote in *Personal Benchmark* (co-authored with Brinker Capital founder Chuck Widger), researchers found the following distinctions between the two crowds:

Of those in a single, traditional investment portfolio:

- 50% chose to fully liquidate their portfolios or at least their equity portfolios, including many high net worth clients who had no immediate need for cash.
- 10% made significant changes in their equity allocation, reducing it by 25% or more.

Of those clients in a goals-based investment strategy:

- 75% made no changes.
- 20% decided to increase the size of their immediate needs pool but left their longer-term assets fully invested.

As Melissa Rayer of SEI concluded, the key finding was that "goals-based investors are less likely to panic and make ill-informed changes to their portfolios."[37] From the vantage of someone in a traditional portfolio, 2008 was a truly horrifying time. They would have seen their total wealth cut nearly in half with no distinction made between short- and long-term needs. It's no wonder that 60% of SEI's investors bailed or greatly reduced their positions!

The goals-based investor, on the other hand, would realize that certain of her goals would be totally unimpacted by the crisis as they were so far down the road. Since most goals-based approaches also include a short-term "safety" bucket, she would have also had the immediate peace of mind necessary to weather the storm. For an approach with such far-reaching impact, goals-based investing is blissfully uncomplicated. By simply breaking our investments into their constituent buckets and labeling them with a purpose, we are able to gain the perspective necessary to ignore volatility in favor of what matters most.

In addition to fighting short-termism, personal benchmarking also draws on the power of what psychologists call "mental accounting". A form of framing, mental accounting says that the way we frame a question (or an account) has much to do with how we will respond. For instance, a *New York Times*/CBS poll on the "Don't Ask Don't Tell" legislation asked the same question framed two different ways and got dramatically different results.[38] The first question asked if "gay men and lesbians" should be allowed to serve openly in the military and 79% of the Democrats polled responded in the affirmative. A second framing of the question asked if respondents were in favor of "homosexuals serving openly in the military", to which a mere 43% of Democrats gave their ascent.

Likewise, studies have shown that people are apt to save money labeled as a rebate but to spend money labeled as a bonus. Barack Obama and his advisors, skilled in the science of behavioral economics, used framing to position the stimulus given out after the Great Recession as a bonus to incent recipients to buy big screen TVs rather than hoard it. The way you label your money has everything to do with how you spend and save it; a tendency that goals-based investing uses to full advantage.

Consider the words of George Loewenstein:

"The process of mentally bucketing money in multiple accounts is often combined with earmarking the accounts for specific goals. While it seems like an inconsequential process, earmarking can have a dramatic effect on retirement savings. Cheema and Soman found that earmarking savings in an envelope labeled with a picture of a couple's children nearly doubled the savings rate of very low income parents."[39]

Abraham Maslow found that we have a hierarchy of needs, with higher order needs contingent on the successful meeting of needs for safety, food and shelter. Likewise, we are best able to focus on higher order financial goals such as leaving a legacy when we have a bucket of assets framed to meet our immediate safety needs. This concept is illustrated in figure 1.

Figure 1—Example hierarchies of financial needs

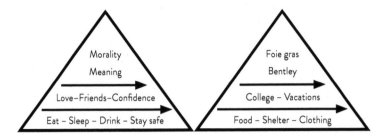

When investments are labeled with respect to the particular need they should meet, both our expected returns and appropriate behavior come into sharper relief. What's more, the process of intentional framing can do much to incent the otherwise painful act of setting aside today's money for tomorrow. Who would have guessed that there is such power in simply naming your money?

The madness of men

Some of my proudest work has been in teaming with Chuck Widger and Brinker Capital to create their goals-based investing platform, Personal Benchmark. Chuck, a long-time proponent of personalized approaches, brought me in to add some science to what he had observed anecdotally for years—the best investors ignore the broader market and focus on getting the returns that they need to live the life they want. For all of the sense that personal benchmarking makes intuitively, it requires us to swim against some deep-seated behavioral currents. As a human race, we are generally more interested in being better than other people than we are in doing well ourselves.

This "crab in a bucket" mentality explains the research of Meir Statman, who found that those he surveyed would prefer to make $50,000 in a community where the average salary is $25,000 than make $100,000 in a community where the average salary is $250,000. Through my work with Brinker we have found that the only force greater than this sort of comparative greed is a focus on the values, convictions and dreams of the client. Discovering these values takes conversations between advisor and client that go far deeper than usual, but the result is a more meaningful journey that pays both behavioral and financial dividends.

The story of Sir Isaac Newton serves as a useful cautionary tale for those who insist on comparative rather than personal benchmarks. Unlike some great thinkers whose genius is discovered posthumously, Newton was celebrated in his day and enjoyed the financial spoils of his notoriety. Seeking to compound his already sizable wealth, Newton invested in the South Sea Company, a British joint-stock company founded as a public-private partnership aimed at reducing the national debt.

In a show of grandiosity, the British government granted the South Sea Company exclusive rights to trade with South America, a distinction made entirely moot by the fact that the continent was controlled by Spain. Unaware of the futility of this "monopoly", speculators bid up the price of the South Sea Company and Newton became richer still, before exiting with both principal and interest squarely in hand. But while Newton had exited early, many of his (far less clever) friends stayed with the stock as the shares continued to soar.

Despite being already financially secure, Newton could not stomach the fact that his friends' and neighbors' wealth was outstripping his own and piled back into the stock shortly before it cratered back to its flotation price. Sir Isaac Newton, the genius scientist with all-too-human tendencies, is quoted after the fact as saying, "I can calculate the movement of the stars, but not the madness of men."

Keeping score is natural, but there are adaptive and maladaptive ways in which to do so. Benchmarking outside of ourselves furthers a petty competitiveness that is not reflective of what we value or need. Conversely, by infusing our investment process with the values that we hold most dear, we are able to secure for ourselves the returns that we need, align our gaze with our long-term investment goals and experience safety in the short term.

As I wrote in *Personal Benchmark*:

"...the investment process becomes arduous when it becomes decoupled from the larger purpose it serves. Even seemingly small investment decisions will take on a dynamism and life of their own when viewed through the appropriate lens. Perhaps making investment decisions will never be the reason you get out of bed in the morning, but whatever does get you out of bed can certainly be at the forefront of how you make decisions."

What now?

Think—"Worry *less* about the economy and more about *your* economy."
Ask—"Does this news matter to me and my situation in particular?"
Do—Bucket (either physically or mentally) your assets relative to your deeply held ambitions and long-term financial goals.

Rule #7

Forecasting Is For Weathermen

"Those who have knowledge don't predict. Those who predict don't have knowledge."

—Lao Tzu

Worst. Genie. Ever.

IMAGINE FOR A moment that you are an archaeologist in a far-off land, once populated by a sophisticated race of people rumored to have been in possession of magical powers. You are here to unearth the relics of their mysticism and, being the skeptic that you are, disprove this arcane obsession with the supernatural.

In the process of gingerly picking through some ancient ruins, you discover a lamp. Being a fan of Disney movies from the '90s, you decide to give it a rub. To your surprise, a genie emerges, but sadly he informs you he is not of the "any three wishes you desire" variety but rather of the "two pre-loaded options" variety. Just your luck—your skeptical worldview has been shattered and you get a bum genie. Nevertheless, a wish is a wish and you inquire as to your two options. The genie then informs you that you can have either $30,000 given to you each year for life, or sufficient free time to take a 30-minute walk every day. Strange options to be sure—but which do you think would bring you more happiness?

If you are like most people (and certainly like me) you choose the money. After all, the impact of $30,000 a year over a lifetime is substantial. However, research shows that while our brains tell us that money will make us happier, the regular exercise does far more to improve happiness and quality of life.[40]

How can we misforecast something so simple? After all, we interact with money and walking with some regularity. Shouldn't we be better programmed to understand their impact on our wellbeing? It turns out that we are quite good at forecasting what will cause us physical pain (e.g., getting punched in the face) or pleasure (e.g., food, sex), but have a very limited capacity to forecast psychological utility.

As Dan Gilbert astutely observes in his TED talk, the reason there isn't such a thing as liver and onion flavored ice cream is not because a focus group was held and deemed it unsavory—it's because we know intuitively it would taste gross.[41] Psychologically, however, we fall prey to a host of cognitive distortions that lead us to miscalibrate what brings us joy and sadness. And if these distortions stymie our individual efforts to forecast the familiar, they make forecasting the actions of a dynamic human system like the stock market just about impossible. To quote Nassim Taleb, "Our track record in figuring out significant rare events in politics and economics is not close to zero; it is zero."[42]

Perhaps we have had little collective success in forecasting the black swans studied by Taleb, but what about the track record of more mundane types of financial forecasting? This is important knowledge because, as James Montier asserts, between 80% and 90% of active investment managers make their decisions on a forecast-based model.[43]

Famed investor James O'Shaughnessy describes the process as so: "most common is for a person to run through a variety of possible outcomes in his or her head, essentially relying on personal knowledge, experience, and common sense to reach a decision. This is known as a clinical or intuitive approach, and it is how most traditional active money managers make choices... This type of judgment relies on the perceptiveness of the forecaster."[44] It all sounds sensible enough, until you realize that we are relying on the perceptiveness of forecasters that as a whole are not at all perceptive.

Contrarian investor David Dreman found that most (59%) Wall Street "consensus" forecasts miss their targets by gaps so large as to make the results unusable—either under or overshooting the actual number by more than 15%.[45] Further analysis by Dreman found that from 1973 to 1993, the nearly 80,000 estimates he looked at had a mere 1 in 170 chance of being within 5% of the actual number.[46]

James Montier sheds some light on the difficulty of forecasting in his *Little Book of Behavioral Investing*. In 2000 the average target price of stocks was 37% above market price and they ended up 16%. In 2008 the average forecast was a 28% increase and the market fell 40%. Between 2000 and 2008, analysts failed to even get the direction right in four out of the nine years. Finally, Michael Sandretto of Harvard and Sudhir Milkrishnamurthi of MIT looked at the one-year forecasts of the 1000 companies covered most widely by analysts. They found that the analysts were consistently inconsistent, missing the mark by an annual rate of 31.3% on average.[47] The research is unequivocal— forecasts don't work. As a corollary, neither does investing based on these forecasts.

Confidently incompetent

You might think that the bad news about forecasting couldn't get any worse, but you'd be wrong. Not only are forecasters bad in aggregate, but the worst forecasters of all are the ones we are most likely to tune in to. Philip Tetlock of UCLA performed the most exhaustive study of expert forecasts to date, examining 82,000 predictions over 25 years by 300 experts. The overarching conclusion of the study is what you might now expect—"expert" forecasts barely edge out flipping a coin. More damning still were Tetlock's other findings, that the more confidence an expert had, the worse his predictions tended to be and that the more famous an expert was, the worse her predictions were on average. Only in Wall Street Bizarro World would we expect confident experts to be stupid and famous thought leaders to be deserving of infamy.

Let's take a moment to consider the mechanics of how confidence and fame get turned on their heads in the world of financial forecasting. Consider the pedigree of a rock star forecaster: she has a PhD in Financial Engineering from Harvard, holds the hard-won distinction of being a Chartered Financial Analyst (CFA), and has scratched and clawed her way to the top of the heap at Goldman Sachs. Given the unfairness of life, she is likely also a marathoner, concert pianist, accomplished chef and all-round ass kicker.

To put it mildly, most financial experts are smart, wealthy, successful and used to getting their way. In the face of such widespread prowess, it becomes easy to see how a sort of boldness emerges. As Dr. Brian Portnoy says, "...precisely because they know so much about a particular subject—they are comfortable offering bold predictions." But this boldness leads to hubris that begets poor results for those heeding their advice.[48]

When Tetlock's "experts" were asked to rate their confidence, those who asserted having over 80% confidence in their opinion were still right less than half of the time.[49] Worst of all, when informed of their inaccuracy, forecasters had a predictable set of excuses (e.g., "It just hasn't happened yet!") that kept them from improving the quality of their prognostications going forward.

Confidence appears to be a hindrance to effective forecasting, but what are we to make of Tetlock's finding that the most famous experts tended to have the least accurate forecasts? Given the sheer number of market forecasters and the limited range of possibilities from which to choose, there are bound to be winners each year that correctly forecast even three standard deviation type outcomes. Typically, these improbable calls are made by either perma-bears or perma-bulls whose constant and typically unchanging thesis happens to align periodically with the facts of the day. Many of those who "called" the 2008 financial crisis had been calling for just such a crisis for years, making them more like the proverbial broken clock that is right twice a day than any sort of financial prophet.

Nevertheless, the financial press is always looking for a seer and exposure tends to follow those who make dramatic calls. Having built a career on the strength of a black swan call, the newly crowned market prophets tend to—you guessed it—keep making bold predictions, typically similar to the one that made them famous to begin with. The problem with this approach is twofold; markets tend to be fairly boring on average and the causes of the last crisis tend to have little in common with the seeds of the next crisis. By always fighting the last war and making dramatic calls in undramatic times, the world's most famous experts tend to underperform their less prominent colleagues.

Perverse incentives

We now know that financial forecasting is an exercise in futility that is only made worse by fame and overconfidence. But if we are to come up with an alternative to relying on forecast-based investing advice, we must first examine some of the structural impediments that make forecasting so difficult. Chief among these is that Wall Street analysts are not paid for the accuracy of their forecasts and often have perverse incentives to mislead investors.

Dartmouth professor Kent L. Womack found that analysts in the early 1990s were making about six "buy" recommendations for every one "sell" call on the stocks they covered. But by the turn of the century, that ratio had ballooned to nearly 50 "buys" for every sell rating.[50] Instead of warning investors against the rising tide of euphoria that created the Tech Wreck, the analysts even helped to further that mania by acting in their own self-interests. Cusatis and Woolridge found that nearly a third of all firms have negative long-term earnings, meaning that accurate forecasts would require analysts to issue "sell" calls on around one-third of all stocks at any given time. In reality, the number of firms projected by analyst calls to have negative earnings is 17/100 of 1%.[51]

If this systematic bias toward optimism were just part of our frail psychology it might be forgiven. Sadly though, the reasons for this buy tilt are baked into the very way in which the game is played. If forecasting is hard for reasons all its own, it is made impossible in practice by the way that Wall Street analysts are rewarded. Joel Greenblatt explains the process:

"Another occupational hazard for research analysts is that analysts who pan a company's stock are usually cut off from an important source of information. Crucial contact with company officers and information from investor-relations personnel may well be reserved for other, more 'cooperative' analysts. The vast majority of analysts are not directly paid by clients. The research recommendations and reports produced by these analysts are peddled by the firm's stockbrokers in exchange for commission business. One perennial problem is the overwhelming incentive for analysts to issue 'Buy' recommendations."[52]

To recap: analysts are supposed to issue dispassionate buy and sell recommendations in appropriate measure, but work for companies who profit from a "buy" call and make no money on a "sell". What's more, the companies themselves may withhold the very information needed to make an honest appraisal if the analyst does not pre-commit to cooperate. Imagine a weatherman paid on sales of umbrellas or a baseball umpire allowed to bet on games and you will have an excellent analogy to the murky incentives of a financial analyst.

Nearly 100 years ago, Alfred Cowles conducted one of the first studies on the efficacy of financial forecasting, intuitively titled, 'Can Stock Market Forecasters Forecast?' In his results, Cowles found that only one-third of forecasters could do their job: namely, pick market-beating stocks over the course of a five-year period.[53] As Charles Ellis says, "forecasting the future of any variable is difficult, forecasting the interacting futures of many changing variables is more difficult, and estimating how other expert investors interpret such complex changes is extraordinarily difficult."[54]

Ellis's comments are true in a vacuum and are made increasingly so by the fact that egos have gotten bigger and incentives more convoluted in the time since Cowles did his work. In my estimation, the entire Wall Street forecasting-industrial-complex could be done away with today with zero harm, and indeed much good, accruing to the individual investor. Why then, in the face of such damning evidence, do we continue to listen?

Cognitive cruise control

Ben Graham was on to something when he said, "nearly everyone interested in common stocks wants to be told by someone else what he thinks the market is going to do. The demand being there, it must be supplied."[55] But this is more than just a misguided case of supply chasing demand. It turns out that our brains long for forecasts in a very specific way. Of all of the metabolic demands made on your body, the brain is the greediest, gobbling up as much as 20% of all of the calories you take in. The body being an efficient machine, it is always looking for ways to conserve energy and nothing provides as big a return as slowing down the brain.

This is born out by MRI studies that show listening to financial experts shuts off some brain functions. Such cognitive respite may be desirable for parsimonious bodily functioning, but it is detrimental to making money. The scientists in the study examined brain activity while making financial decisions under a number of conditions. When participants were provided with the ideas of a financial expert, the parts of their brain associated with higher order reasoning were less active.

To be as concrete as possible: when you start listening to Jim Cramer, you stop thinking. Just as a professional bicyclist might slipstream a competitor to save energy for a final climb, the brain aches to coast on the ideas of others, effectively going into energy saver mode.

It is discomfiting to understand that your hard-earned money is being put at risk based on stories, rooted in human irrationality, embedded within a rigged system. Scarier still is the observation of Amos Tversky that, "It's frightening to think that you might not know something, but more frightening to think that, by and large, the world is run by people who have faith that they know exactly what's going on." It is unrealistically nihilistic to assume that there is nothing that can be known about stocks that can give you a probabilistic edge in making financial decisions. Conversely, it is unrealistically optimistic to assume that anyone, no matter how worldly or educated, is able to predict the future with any useful degree of certainty.

The middle ground between these two approaches must scrupulously avoid conjecture about the future, rely on systems rather than biased human judgment and be diversified enough to show appropriate humility. It is an approach that says, "I can know some things, but I'll never know everything," and while it's likely to make you some money, it will never land you a spot on CNBC. As you have learned in this chapter, there may not be a crystal ball out there, but that doesn't mean there aren't any handrails.

What now?

Think—"This person has no clue. This person has no clue. This person has no clue."

Ask—"Is this projection probabilistic, measured and research-based? What is this person's prior history of prognostication?"

Do—Act consistently on timeless behavioral principles (see Part Two) rather than guesses about an unknowable future.

Rule #8

Excess Is Never Permanent

"Many shall be restored that are now fallen, and many shall fall that now are in honor."

—**Horace**

Truer words were never spoken

YOU HAVE DOUBTLESS heard the phrase "this too shall pass", but may not be aware of its rich history and hazy origins. The roots of the phrase are attributed to sources as diverse as King Solomon, Sufi poets and more generically to an "Eastern monarch".

In the works of Sufi poets, it is inscribed on a ring given to a king who asked his wise men to create a ring that would make him happy when he felt sad. Of course, the great irony is that a ring inscribed with "this too shall pass" not only made the king happy when he was sad, but had the unintended consequence of making him sad when he was happy. Jewish folklore casts Solomon as both receiver and purveyor of the knowledge of impermanence, with one story describing the phrase as the only thing that can truly be said at any given time.

The phrase also enjoyed some popularity in the West in the 19th century and was famously used by Abraham Lincoln who said, "It is said an Eastern monarch once charged his wise men to invent him a sentence, to be ever in view, and which should be true and appropriate in all times and situations. They presented him the words 'This too shall pass away.' How much it expresses! How chastening in the hour of pride! How consoling in the depths of affliction!"[56]

While the correct genesis of this truism may be unclear, its applicability to investing is undeniable. Investors would be wise to learn the truth that excesses of all kinds are never permanent.

Is *Sports Illustrated* a jinx?

Sports fans everywhere are familiar with what is colloquially referred to as the *Sports Illustrated* cover jinx. The jinx, it is rumored, is that teams or athletes who appear on the front cover of S.I. are doomed to injury, underperformance and downright bad luck in the weeks and months that follow their fame. In late 2003, the Cubs and the Red Sox, two teams with championship droughts nearly a century long, appeared on the cover of *Sports Illustrated* in the midst of what had heretofore been successful playoff runs. Both teams went on to suffer dramatic collapses as the Yankees rallied from a three game deficit to best the Red Sox, and the Cubs lost in seven games to the upstart Marlins.

Michael Spinks graced the cover of *S.I.* before his fight with Mike Tyson with the headline, "Don't Count Me Out." Sadly, Spinks was counted out and knocked out after a mere 91 seconds in the ring with Tyson. The Yankees "Core Four" of Derek Jeter, Mariano Rivera, Andy Pettitte and Jorge Posada appeared in a summer 2010 edition of *S.I.* and, within seven days, all but Jeter had been moved to the disabled list. Spared from injury, Jeter went on to have the worst offensive year of his career.[57]

Fans being the superstitious lot that they are, many want to believe there is some true voodoo in the *Sports Illustrated* jinx. The far more probable explanation, however, is what psychologists refer to as mean reversion, or the tendency of observations to move toward average over time. A team or players merit inclusion on the cover of *Sports Illustrated* by virtue of well-above-average performance. It makes sense that over time their performance will look more ordinary.

In *Thinking, Fast and Slow*, Daniel Kahneman gives the example of working with the Israeli Air Force and hearing one leader observe that every time an airman executed a perfect move, he would receive significant praise from his higher ups, only to have his performance suffer on the next run. It was this leader's assumption that the praise was the source of the underperformance, that somehow it might make the airmen weak or complacent. Kahneman was later able to prove empirically that regardless of praise or criticism, really exceptional runs tended to be followed by worse performance and that really awful runs would likely be followed by improved performance. Positive or negative feedback were smokescreens for what truly mattered—the tendency of performance to look average over time.

Francis Galton, an English statistician, found the same thing in his study of heredity. Exceptionally tall people tended to have shorter children and very intelligent people tended to have offspring that skewed more average as well, something he referred to as "regression toward mediocrity." Whether studying human intelligence, athletic prowess, or the length of beanstalks, as Daniel Kahneman remarked to Amos Tversky, "Once you become sensitized to it, you see regression everywhere."[58]

The impact of regression to the mean can be felt at least as dramatically on Wall Street as it can in Yankee Stadium, although it is little understood by the average investor. James O'Shaughnessy spoke to its power when he said, "the most ironclad rule I have been able to find studying masses of data on the stock market, both in the United States and developed foreign markets, is the idea of reversion to the mean."[59]

As you are now painfully aware, the rules of Wall Street Bizarro World have little to do with our lived experience elsewhere. It is human nature to expect observations to remain relatively unchanged. We expect if we meet a person we find kind and considerate today, that they will be equally so one year from now. Likewise, we expect that if a business is well-run and profitable today this excellence will persist. It is just this expectation of constancy in a world that is perpetually crashing toward its average that can lead investors to make poor decisions in times of both extreme optimism and pessimism. We are wired to expect consistency—of our athletes and our stocks—but live in a world in which extremes tend to be quickly extinguished.

Jim Collins and Jerry Porras' book *Built to Last* is one of the most widely-read and critically acclaimed business books in circulation. It is based on research conducted over a six-year period "to identify underlying characteristics that are common to highly visionary companies" and to communicate those to the broader business world. Basically, Collins and Porras wanted to examine the best companies around and distill the essence of what made them great.

In the ten years before the publication of *Built to Last*, the visionary companies featured in the book soundly outperformed the S&P 500, returning 21% versus 17.5% from the broader market.[60] This outperformance makes sense given that their performance was presumably a part of what merited including them in a book on business excellence. However, we quickly see the effects of mean reversion creeping in, as only half of the featured companies outperformed the broad market in the five years following the study. If we make our examination of these visionary companies broader still (from 1991 to 2007), we see that they actually underperform the S&P 500, providing a 13% annualized return compared to 14% for the index. In business excellence as elsewhere, this too shall pass.

What we observe with the individual companies featured in Built to Last is seen in aggregate studies of winners and losers, as well as studies of fund managers. A study conducted by the Brandes Institute found that even the very best long-term fund managers showed lengthy periods of underperformance, typically followed by sharp reversion to the mean. At some point in the study, the best managers trailed their benchmark by nearly 20% on average. Even at three-year periods, nearly 40% of the best managers were listed in the bottom decile of performance.[61] The "best manager" strategies that had formerly been out of favor tended to show 17% per annum outperformance over the next seven years, but all too often these managers had been abandoned by their investors, who were not around to realize the subsequent outperformance.

In 1998, Larry Summers of Harvard and James Porterba of MIT published a seminal paper titled 'Mean Reversion in Stock Prices: Evidence and Implications'. They set out to examine the returns to NYSE stocks from 1926 to 1985, to understand the after-effects of large increases or decreases in price. As you may now expect, they found that periods of exceptionally high returns were followed by periods of low returns and vice versa. Likewise, Richard Thaler and Werner DeBondt found in their paper 'Does the Stock Market Overreact?' that winner stocks eventually went on to be losers and that today's losers tended to be tomorrow's winners. They examined the 35 best performing stocks of the past five years versus the worst performing duds. They found that over the medium term (17 months), the former loser stocks outperformed the index by 17%, whereas the former darlings underperformed the index by 6%.

Nothing gold can stay

We touched briefly before on the human need for constancy and how it can translate into the mistaken belief that the future will look much like the present. Just as we assume that a kind friend today will be a kind friend one year from now, we also mistakenly suppose that today's hot sector will grow unabated into the future. But as Kenneth Boulding famously said, "Anyone who thinks steady growth can continue indefinitely is either a madman or an economist."

It was just this sort of over-optimistic projection that caused the Japanese real estate market to bubble up in the late 1980s. At one point, the real estate market in just Toyko was worth four times as much as all of the real estate in the United States![62] At one manic peak in the London Stock Exchange, it grew 100 times in value in 25 years, valuing it at more than five times all of the cash in Europe.[63] Similarly, as James O'Shaughnessy reports of the US tech bubble, "…companies like Constellation 3D, eNotes.com, simplayer.com and Braintech saw their stock price appreciate by more than 1000% despite having zero sales."[64]

A failure to account for the impermanence of excess is the pump that inflates bubbles that eventually cause lengthy and widespread destruction of real wealth. A savvy investor, like a wise Eastern monarch, must wear the ring that provides solace in times of despair and humility in times of plenty.

It is painful to admit to oneself that every period of economic prosperity has within it the manic seeds of the next crash. Contrary to the popular idea of bear markets being risky and bull markets being risk-free, the behavioral investor must concede that risk is actually created in periods of market euphoria and actualized in down markets.

Another difficulty in clearly assessing excess is that many periods of elevated market sentiment are birthed by true ideas that are taken to the extreme. The tech bubble of the turn of the century was predicated on the assumption that the internet would change the way we do business, a belief that is truer today than most could have imagined at the time! However, it did not mean that business realities like profitability would give way to more ethereal measures of valuation like "mindshare" or "eyeballs on the page".

Just as air travel has revolutionized our world but airlines have been disappointing stocks, there are innovations present in the market today that will change the way we live but prove to be unwise investments given our human tendency toward unrealistic enthusiasm. As Ben Graham said, "Obvious prospects for physical growth in a business do not translate into obvious profits for investors."[65] The very fact that most periods of financial excess are born from a kernel of truth makes them so very hard to identify.

Mark Twain shrewdly noted that history does not repeat itself, but it does rhyme. The next episode of excessive fear or greed won't look quite like the last, but it will have in common an unrealistic expectation that tomorrow will look exactly like today and that "this time is different." As financial historian J. K. Galbraith says in *A Short History of Financial Euphoria*:

"When the same or closely similar circumstances occur again, sometimes in only a few years, they are hailed by a new, often youthful, and always supremely self-confident generation as a brilliantly innovative discovery in the financial and larger economic world. There can be few fields of human endeavor in which history counts for so little as in the world of finance. Past experience, to the extent that is part of memory at all, is dismissed as the primitive refuge of those who do not have the insight to appreciate the incredible wonders of the present."[66]

Recognizing this excess, frankly, will require you to be a bit of a wet blanket. You will seem out of step at all times, a dogged optimist in the face of global gloom and a cautious historian in a time of champagne and roses. It's not fun, but it can be profitable.

When Warren Buffett wrote his now-famous, 'Buy American' op-ed in 2008, he was not making a market call and conceded that he had no idea what would happen to the market in the short term. He was merely keeping perspective and repeating the one phrase that is never outmoded, "this too shall pass away."

What now?

Think—"This too shall pass."

Ask—"Has the belief that the future will look just like the present opened up opportunities to buy quality businesses at low prices?"

Do—Prepare your finances for famine in times of feast and feast in times of famine.

Rule #9

Diversification Means Always Having To Say You're Sorry

"I suppose my formula might be: dream, diversify and never miss an angle."

—Walt Disney

I F YOU'RE EVER desirous to feel as though you are impossibly poor, take a look at the Forbes 400 list of the richest people in America. Once the jealousy has subsided, view the list with an eye to what its members have in common.

At first glance nothing may stand out. Some, like Oprah Winfrey, come from humble beginnings, whereas others, like Donald Trump, inherited a small fortune at a young age. They are black and white, male and female, young and old, but keep looking and you'll notice one thing—most of them became extravagantly rich from a concentrated position, typically in a single company. Whether it's Bill Gates and Microsoft, Warren Buffett and Berkshire Hathaway, or Mark Zuckerberg and Facebook, they are not very well diversified. If concentration is the sine qua non of ridiculous wealth, how then can I (and every financial professional you have ever met) possibly tout the merits of diversification? It's because while concentration is the fastest way to impossibly high levels of wealth, it is also the fast train to low levels of wealth. Get rich fast and get poor fast are opposing sides of the same coin.

Harry Markowitz gets most of the credit for popularizing diversification across asset classes in financial circles, but the understanding of diversification as a behavioral tool is ancient. The Bible mentions the benefits of diversification as a risk management technique in *Ecclesiastes* (11:2), a book estimated to have been written around 935 BC. It reads: "But divide your investments among many places, for you do not know what risks might lie ahead."

The *Talmud* too references an early form of diversification, the prescription there being to split one's assets into three parts—one third in business, another third in currency and the final third in real estate. The most famous, and perhaps most eloquent, early mention of diversification is found in Shakespeare's *The Merchant of Venice*, where we read:

"My ventures are not in one bottom trusted, Nor to one place, nor is my whole estate Upon the fortune of this present year: Therefore, my merchandise makes me not sad."

It is interesting to note how these early mentions of diversification focus as much on psychology as they do on the financial benefits of diversification, for investing broadly is as much about managing fear and uncertainty as it is concerned with making money. At its essence, diversification is applied humility in the face of an uncertain future. I think of diversification much the same way that insurers think of providing coverage. Just as some insured folks will have accidents that trigger a payout every year, many more will not. Insurance companies make money because their risk is diversified across the corpus of those paying premiums. Similarly, when you are diversified between and within asset classes, the failure of one single type of investment does not dramatically diminish your odds of long-term success.

If my insurance analogy leaves you cold, Ben Carlson suggests thinking of diversification as a form of regret minimization. As he says in *A Wealth of Common Sense*, "Some investors will regret missing out on huge gains while others will regret participating in huge losses. Which regret will wear worse on your emotions?"[67]

Now, before you answer, let me say that the research suggests fairly unequivocally that you will regret participating in losses more than you will regret missing out on huge gains. Daniel Kahneman and Amos Tversky found when examining the utility curve for gains and losses that we hate losing far more than we love winning. Tennis star Andre Agassi put this into words well when he said, "Now that I've won a slam, I know something very few people on earth are permitted to know. A win doesn't feel as good as a loss feels bad, and the good feeling doesn't last as long as the bad. Not even close."

Perhaps you are the rare breed of human that feels the pain of missed gains more than the pain of realized losses. In that case, get uber-concentrated and prepare for a wild ride. But if you're like the rest of us, diversification goes a long way toward decreasing volatility en route to meeting our long-term financial goals.

Humility in practice

Take, for example, the "Lost Decade" of the early aughts, thusly named because investors in large capitalization US stocks (e.g., the S&P 500) would have realized losses of 1% per annum over that ten-year stretch. Ouch. Those who were evenly diversified across five asset classes (US stocks, foreign stocks, commodities, real estate, and bonds), however, didn't experience a lost decade at all, realizing a respectable annualized gain of 7.2% per year. Other years, the shoe is on the other foot. Over the seven years following the Great Recession, stocks exploded upward while a diversified basket of assets had more tepid growth. In fact, you can take it to the bank that some of your assets will underperform every single year, a reality acknowledged in Dr. Brian Portnoy's phrase, "diversification means always having to say you're sorry."

The simple fact is that no one knows which asset classes will do well at any given time and diversification is the only logical response to such uncertainty. For instance, stocks and bonds have only been down in the same year three times since 1928 (1931, 1941 and 1969), meaning that their mutual presence serves as a buffer in tough times.[68] Just as an airbag is a useless expense until you get in a wreck, bonds are a drag on performance—until they aren't.

But conceding to uncertainty does not have to mean compromising returns. In fact, broad diversification and rebalancing have been shown to add half a percentage point of performance per year, a number that can seem small until you realize how it is compounded over an investment lifetime.[69] Take, for example, the case of European, Pacific and US Stocks cited in *A Wealth of Common Sense*. From 1970 to 2014, the annualized returns were as follows:

- European stocks: 10.5%
- Pacific stocks: 9.5%
- US stocks: 10.4%

Similar returns, but let's examine what happens when all three markets are combined, equally weighted and rebalanced each year-end to maintain consistent portfolio composition. In what can only be described as a diversification miracle, the average return of the portfolio over this time is 10.8% annualized—greater than any of its individual parts! Each market had good years and bad years and the automatic rebalancing has the effect of selling winners and buying losers. *Buying low and selling high*—sound familiar? By entering when stocks were cheap and exiting when they became more expensive, the synergistic effects of diversification are realized.

In addition to the benefits of diversification already mentioned, owning a number of asset classes tends to tamp down volatility, which in turn reduces "variance drain". Variance drain sounds heady, but in a nutshell it refers to the detrimental effects of compounding wealth off of lower lows when investing in a highly volatile manner. Even when arithmetic means are the same, the impact on accumulated wealth can be dramatic.

OK, so it's still heady! Let's take an example to show how this works. Say you invest $100,000 each in two products that both average 10% returns per year, one with great volatility and the other with managed volatility. The managed volatility money rises 10% for each of two years, yielding a final result of $121,000. The more volatile investment returns

–20% in year one and a whopping 40% in year two, also resulting in a similar 10% average yearly gain.

The good news is that you can brag to your golf buddies about having achieved a 40% return—you are an investment wizard! The bad news, however, is that your investment will sit at a mere $112,000, fully $9000 less than your investment in the less volatile investment since your gains compounded off of lower lows. Very few investors understand that it takes a 100% gain to recoup from a 50% loss. The value of diversification is largely that it smoothes the ride, resulting in greater compounded wealth and an experience less susceptible to bad investor behavior.

Chart 2—Lifetime returns for individual US stocks

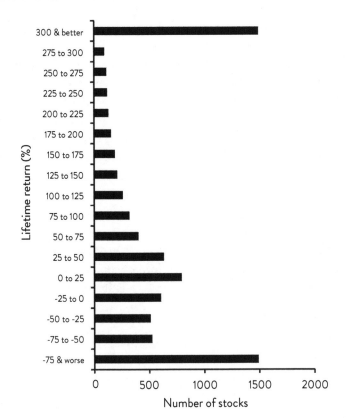

I said at the outset of this chapter that the common thread uniting the ultra-wealthy of all stripes was an extremely concentrated portfolio, one stock in many cases. Perhaps you would like to pick just one stock as you have visions of driving a Maserati, indefinitely forgoing water for champagne and hiring a manservant named Clarence. Well, before you pop that Cristal, let me encourage you to look at the results of a study conducted by Longboard Asset Management. Longboard found that nearly 40% of stocks lose money over their lifetime, 64% underperform a broad market index and one-quarter of stocks account for basically all of the gains in the market over time. This research is shown in chart 2.

It is seductive to think of how your wealth would have exploded had you bet it all on (insert favorite story stock here), but history tells us that the odds are twice as great that you'll go broke on a single stock as you will hit it big. For now, it's probably best to drink water, do your own dishes, drive that Camry and, above all, diversify.

It's a small world after all

Having hopefully now convinced you of the importance of diversification, let me deliver a bit of bad news—it's getting harder to do. Like anything, globalization has had its pros (blending of cultural traditions, increased empathy) and cons (nationalism, destruction of indigenous cultures), but its impact on our best efforts at diversification is undeniable.

In a world that is increasingly connected, it is getting more and more difficult to invest in assets that are truly uncorrelated. From 1971 to 1999, the 12-month correlation between the S&P 500 and the MSCI EAFE (the index of world shares, excluding the US) was 0.42. From the turn of the century on it has averaged 0.83![70] According to Tang and Xiong, commodities have suffered a similar loss of uniqueness.[71] Throughout the 1990s and early 2000s, the average one-year correlation among indexed commodities remained at about 0.10. By 2009 it had quintupled in value to 0.50! Worse still, the correlation between commodities and equities rocketed to 0.80 during the financial crisis of 2008, losing their power to diversify just as it was most needed.[72]

As the world continues to shrink and our interdependence grows, it seems intuitive to suggest that asset classes of all sorts will look more and more like one another. The basic tenets of diversification within and among asset classes are timeless and will continue to serve investors well, but within this larger framework, investors will need to seek out new sources of uncorrelated returns.

Studies of ethnically and psychologically diverse (i.e., having varied personality types) corporate teams have yielded some fascinating results. Diverse teams take longer to make decisions, argue more and generally have a more circuitous path to performance than less diverse teams. However, they also make better decisions, evaluate a wider range of possibilities and, most importantly, tend to create more profitable businesses.

Likewise, owning a diverse basket of assets or stocks is a certain recipe for disappointment if you take too narrow a view. There will always be laggards and your mind will generate an endless stream of "if only" scenarios that would have been superior to humble diversification. But considered as a whole portfolio over long-periods of time, the power of diversification is so profound that hedge fund titan Cliff Asness calls it "the only free lunch in investing." Diversification may mean always having to say you're sorry, but it's far better than what you'll be saying if you don't diversify.

What now?

Think—"Get rich fast and get poor fast are sides of the same coin."
Ask—"How can I diversify my personal and employment risk by learning new skills and forging new relationships?"
Do—Diversify across asset classes to include domestic equities, foreign equities, fixed income and real estate, at a minimum.

Rule #10
Risk Is Not A Squiggly Line

"October. This is one of the peculiarly dangerous months to speculate in stocks in. The others are July, January, September, April, November, May, March, June, December, August and February."

—Mark Twain, *Pudd'nhead Wilson*

ALTHOUGH I HAVE spent my entire career applying behavioral principles to the world of finance, my PhD is in clinical psychology. As one of the components for completion of my doctoral program, I was required to provide thousands of hours of counseling to clients in crisis, a skill set that has proven invaluable in speaking to panicked investors.

My first ever client (we will call her Brooke, not her real name) is a memorable one and her story provides a valuable vehicle for considering the concept of risk. Brooke entered my office holding six envelopes that she immediately placed on the desk before saying, "I have a problem." Brooke was well dressed, articulate and, I understood from her file, an exceptional student. I frankly couldn't imagine what could be troubling someone so poised. As the session went on, Brooke began to expound upon her problem and I did my best not to look like the scared rookie that I was. Brooke was an aspiring scientist and had applied to a number of prestigious PhD programs, all of which had responded to her via post—these were the six letters presented to me at the outset. She had dreamed of being a scientist since she was a young child, had spent her time at high school in solemn preparation for acceptance to a good college and had been a diligent student throughout her university years. Everything she had ever done had been preparing for this moment!

The letters had arrived and she had done nothing. Having poured so much time and intention into preparing for this moment, she was now faced with the prospect of actually discovering whether or not she had been accepted. With the deadlines for enrollment looming, she had to face her fears, open the envelopes and take action, but she was paralyzed. She could not bear the thought of being rejected at something she had worked so hard to bring about.

Throughout the session, I was a mess. Brooke's presenting concerns had not been covered in any of my textbooks and I was nonplussed that someone so seemingly together could act so erratically. I distinctly remember fumbling over words, actually dropping my files at one point and just generally being useless. I had been taught not to give direct advice, but rather to ask the sort of pointed questions that would help the client arrive at her own solutions. Easier said than done in the moment.

Frustrated with my own inability to lead her in a good direction, I finally blurted out, "It seems to me that by being afraid to take a risk, you're bringing about the inevitability of the very thing you're afraid of." It wasn't pretty, but it worked. Brooke and I both realized that day that our best efforts at managing uncertainty can sometimes bring about certain disappointment—a reality as true in investing as it is in life. And, oh yes, she got into all six schools and had her pick of the lot! Brooke's problem stemmed from a definition of risk that deviated from her lived experience of the concept. Brooke had defined risk as a rejection letter and in her avoidance of the letters altogether, mistakenly supposed that she was avoiding risk.

Risk defined

Definitions matter and investment managers—appropriately concerned about risk—have landed on an asset's volatility as a measure of how risky it is. The advantages of using volatility as a measure of risk are primarily those of parsimony—it is easy to measure, can be factually reported and it lends itself to the creation of elegant (if mostly useless) mathematical models. The primary drawback of using volatility as a stand-in for risk is a big one: it does not actually conform in any meaningful way to what it ought to be measuring.

Legendary value investor Howard Marks described this best: "Academicians settled on volatility as the proxy for risk as a matter of convenience. They needed a number for their calculations that was objective and could be ascertained historically and extrapolated into the future. Volatility fits the bill, and most of the other types of risk do not. The problem with all of this, however, is that I just don't think volatility is the risk most investors care about. Rather than volatility, I think that people decline to make investments primarily because they're worried about a loss of capital or an unacceptably low return. To me, 'I need more upside potential because I'm afraid I could lose money' makes an awful lot more sense than 'I need more upside potential because I'm afraid the price may fluctuate.' No, I'm sure 'risk' is—first and foremost—the likelihood of losing money."[73]

Consider again Warren Buffett, whose famous first rule of investing is "Never lose money" and whose second rule is "Never forget the first rule." By some measures, his Berkshire Hathaway has been incredibly risky inasmuch as its stock has been volatile, losing around 50% four times since 1980 alone. However, Buffett has never actualized any of that risk as he has never sold a single share!

An investor focused on volatility would have bailed on Berkshire many times over the last 35 years. Luckily, The Oracle understands the words of his mentor Benjamin Graham that, "the bona fide investor does not lose money merely because the market price of his holdings declines; hence the fact that a decline may occur does not mean that he is running a true risk of loss."[74]

Merriam-Webster defines risk as the "possibility of loss or injury", so it seems reasonable to define investment risk as the possibility of permanent loss of capital. Getting a little closer to home, it would be intuitive to define our personal investment risk as the possibility that we will not be able to live the financial lives we desire. The standard definition of risk as volatility is impersonal but we understand intuitively that risk is contextual. Just as we all have different goals, fears and obligations with respect to money, we all have different risks.

Bearing this in mind, let's see how risky stocks have been with respect to our improved definitions—the possibility of permanent loss of capital and the ability to help us meet our financial goals.

A risk by any other name

We discussed the risk-fighting power of diversification in the last chapter and it must be stated plainly that buying one single stock is a risky proposition indeed. According to J.P. Morgan, 40% of stocks have suffered "catastrophic losses" since 1980, meaning that they fell by 70% or more!

But what happens when we pool those risky individual names into a diversified portfolio? Jeremy Siegel found in *Stocks for the Long Run* that in every rolling 30-year period from the late 1800s to 1992, stocks outperformed both bonds and cash. In rolling ten-year periods, stocks beat cash over 80% of the time and there was never a rolling 20-year period in which stocks lost money. Bonds and cash, considered safe by volatility-based measures of risk, actually failed to keep up with inflation most of that time.

As Siegel says of this twisted logic, "You have never lost money in stocks over any 20-year period, but you have wiped out half your portfolio in bonds [after inflation]. So which is the riskier asset?"[75] Over the past 30-year rolling periods stocks have returned 7.4% after inflation on average whereas bonds have barely kept up, clocking a real return of just 1.4%.[76] I'm not sure what you'd call an asset class that outperforms by an average of 500% a year and does so with great consistency, but I wouldn't call it risky.

Another danger to the volatility-based notion of risk is that it keeps us mired in the day-to-day gyrations of the market instead of focused on the long term. Once again, stocks do seem very scary if you're looking at them every day. Greg Davies shows that if you check your account daily, you'll experience a loss just over 41% of the time. Pretty scary when we consider that human nature makes losses feel about twice as bad as gains feel good! Look once every five years and you would have only experienced a loss about 12% of the time and those peeking every 12 years would never have seen a loss.[77] Twelve years may seem like a long time, but it's worth remembering that the investment lifetime for most individuals is likely to be from 40 to 60 years.

By referring to volatility as a proxy for risk, we forsake the likelihood of long-term compounding for a focus on the unknowable and meaningless meanderings of daily trends. Fund manager Tom Howard says of this fallacy, "One of the ironies is that, by focusing on short-term volatility when building long-horizon portfolios, it is almost certain that investment risk increases."[78]

Long-term investing demands equally long-term measures of risk. Considered against an appropriate timeline, a portfolio with equities as its primary driver provides a great deal of reward with very little risk in the most meaningful sense of the word.

Less sexy, more important

Most investors understand intuitively that managing risk is important, but few understand that the management of downside is even more important than the pursuit of upside. As Howard Marks puts it, "Over a full career, most investors' results will be determined more by how many losers they have, and how bad they are, than by the greatness of their winners. Skillful risk control is the mark of the superior investor."[79]

Notwithstanding its centrality, there are a few characteristics of investment risk that make it difficult to manage. First off, risk exists entirely in the future and, as we have already determined, we are not very skilled at divining what will happen down the road.

A second difficulty is that we don't always receive direct feedback about how successful our efforts at risk management have been. Consider a weatherman who forecasts an 80% chance of rain and advises you to bring an umbrella. Although we don't typically think of it this way, it is possible for it not to rain tomorrow and still have the weatherman be right. After all, he forecast a four-in-five chance, which may well have been the accurate probability even if the dreaded storm never materialized. Short of a "this will never happen" or "this will always happen", it is hard to know if our efforts at risk-management are well placed.

If risk is important to securing great returns but invisible to the eye, what then are we to do?

Peter Bernstein gives us a clue in *Against the Gods*, perhaps the most comprehensive consideration of financial risk ever written. Bernstein suggests, "The essence of risk management lies in maximizing the areas where we have some control over the outcome while minimizing the areas where we have absolutely no control over the outcome and the linkage between effect and cause is hidden from us."[80]

We begin to manage risk by controlling the controllable. Once again, this sensible admonition from Bernstein shows the inadequacy of volatility-based measures of risk. The beta, or volatility of a stock relative to a benchmark, is wildly inconsistent over time and offers us little to hold on to. More fundamental factors, on the other hand, offer both logical and empirical proof that steps toward managing risk can be taken by viewing a stock as what it truly is—a partial share of an actual company—rather than a dot that bounces around on a screen. The more able we are to conceptualize investing in this way, the better able we will be to anticipate potential risks.

One such fundamental consideration is the price paid for a company. Let me say emphatically, there is no greater risk than overpaying for a stock. The riskiness of investing in a given business cannot and should not ever be separated from the price that is paid for it—appropriate valuation work is the core of risk management. From 1950 to 2007, value stocks outperformed both glamour stocks and the broader market benchmarks, and did so with less volatility. By traditional or behavioral measures of risk, not overpaying is the safest move you can make.

To further explore the other sorts of fundamental areas you can look at to assess the risk, let's imagine an investment decision in that greatest of all businesses—the neighborhood lemonade stand. If you were asked to invest in a lemonade stand, what are some of the questions you might ask? You might want to know about the deliciousness of the product, the singularity of a special recipe, the profit margins, the quality of the management or the cost of lemons. There is very little chance that your first question would be, "What has been the volatility of the valuation of the company over time?"

Likewise, when assessing the riskiness of a given stock purchase, we are well served to examine the fundaments of the business rather than the fickle sentiment of outsiders. This can be done by running through a qualitative checklist, such as the following:

- Is there a history of performance here (typically more than five years)?
- Is there a catalyst?
- Is the leadership trustworthy?
- Would I buy the whole company if I could?
- Are there close substitutes for this product or service?
- Do they enjoy pricing power in tough times?
- Is it priced such that there is a margin of safety?
- Why have others overlooked this stock?
- Is it dependent on a union or favorable regulatory conditions?
- Does the brand inspire loyalty?

All of these questions allow the investor to think through possible pitfalls and assess the prudence of buying a given share, but none of them would be considered risk management questions per se by your typical Wall Streeter. That Wall Street is stuck in a faulty, short-sighted paradigm that views risk as a mathematical reduction is a flaw that can be profitably exploited by the long-term, behavioral investor who understands the real definition of risk.

If I have been ruthless in attacking the idea of volatility as the primary measure of risk, it is only because I see the damage that it does to ordinary investors and savers. Volatility is scary in the short term but it loses its sting when we truly understand its place. Since 1871, the market has risen or fallen more than 20% two out of every five years. Volatility is the norm, not the exception, and it should be planned for and diversified against, but never run from. The sooner you can accept that there will be 10 to 15 bear markets in your lifetime, the sooner you will be able to invest in a way that manages the thing you ought to fear most—the possibility that you will have insufficient funds to live the life of your dreams.

In defense of volatility, Nassim Taleb gives the example of a man who arrives home from work each day precisely at 6 o'clock. If he has engaged in this pattern for some time, his family will begin to worry about his safety, even if he is just five minutes late. On the other hand, consider someone who arrives home around 6 o'clock each night, but might arrive at 5:30pm on some evenings and 6:30pm on others. His volatile arrival means his family won't worry as much if he is a bit late. It will take a significant departure from the norm to cause them to worry.

Insisting on absolute consistency has the paradoxical effect of making things less stable, whereas a "bend not break" approach has a strengthening effect over time. Taleb notes that just as we inject a bit of disease into our bodies to create a vaccine, we must have volatility if we are ever to have true security. "One of life's packages," he says, is "no stability without volatility."[81]

Just like family members returning from work, stock returns have consistently "come home" for the long-term investor, albeit within a fairly tight range. For those who insist on certainty, there are far less variable options than equity investing, but that certainty comes at the cost of failing to retain purchasing power and risking that we will be unable to meet even our basic financial needs in the future. Far from being a synonym for risk, volatility is the means by which the behavioral investor receives an outsized reward for having just a modicum of courage and patience.

What now?

Think—"I am the biggest risk to my long-term wealth creation."
Ask—"Am I controlling the controllable?"
Do—Manage real risk by examining the stability of the businesses you are investing in and never overpaying.

Applying the Rules of Behavioral Self-Management

MY ROUTE HOME from work typically takes me over a winding, hilly pass that is the perfect way to decompress after a long day in the office. Like most of us, I usually drive home more or less unconsciously, but I was recently broken from my trance by a tanker spill that obscured all four lanes of traffic. Searching for a new route, I found myself by the nearest hospital, the largest in the area and an institution with a fine track record.

Passing now between the two main buildings and the monorail that connects them, I saw something most unexpected. There, on a nearby lot, were 13 medical professionals in scrubs, smoking. Doctors and nurses! People who would, upon extinguishing their cigarettes, return to the building and plead with their sick patients to stop smoking. I can say with near-certainty that every one of those 13 professionals knew better and yet they couldn't help themselves. The official name for this is the "knowing-doing gap," but whatever you call it, it is a shame.

I have attempted to inoculate you against bad investment behavior by sharing with you research, anecdotes and ideas that you can refer to when planning your financial life. But inasmuch as I am one of you and just as prone to the knowing-doing gap (I just worked out and then ate Skittles, seriously) I know that these rules alone will never be enough. If knowledge and willpower were all it took, we'd all be skinny and Marlboro would be out of business tomorrow.

Since knowledge alone is not enough, the two most important things you can do are own your behavior and get help. By owning your power (Rule #1) you realize that although you may not control the economy of Greece, you do control your ability to save each month, manage your expenses and take a long-term view. Enlisting outside help (Rule #2) will help you to enact all of the other rules presented here. I cannot say emphatically enough that you could read every book on investing ever written and still achieve horrible results without proper support; the pull of Wall Street Bizarro World is just that strong.

Operating in a world where less is more, the few outsmart the many and the future is more certain than the present will never make sense, but that needn't doom you to low returns. The Rules are your guide to staying sane in what is inherently a crazy-making endeavor.

We now move on to Part Two, which sets forth some processes for investing that benefit from the irrational quirks discussed in Part One.

PART
TWO
Behavioral Investing

"History doesn't repeat itself, but it does rhyme."

—**Mark Twain**

IT'S WORTH REPEATING that there is nothing more predictive of your investment success than your ability to engage in the behaviors mentioned in Part One. Having now been exposed to two handfuls of sound investment behaviors, you could read no further, apply these principles dutifully and beat 90% of investment professionals, to say nothing of your histrionic peers.

But behavioral management is not the only way the savvy investor can amplify returns. Psychology also holds a further key to improving portfolio returns and when paired with the program of sensible behavior from Part One, this can be a formidable one-two punch. Part Two outlines models of behavioral risk management and considerations for security selection that will serve as guardrails for managing your assets, just as surely as the rules of Part One should guide your behavior. I call this model for constraining behavioural risk *rule-based behavioural investing*, or RBI (named for a simultaneous love of baseball and brevity).

This all sounds very exotic from the outset, so let me manage your expectations by telling you just how arduous, boring and commonsensical this all will be. An interesting anecdote from the world of marketing illustrates just how troublesome it can be for us to realize that there is no magic to things that we suppose to be complicated.

As the story goes, Unilever was preparing to launch a new shampoo in Asia when a mischievous marketing employee wrote on the label, "Contains the X9 Factor". The addition of this claim about a fictional element went undetected by Unilever executives and millions of bottles were produced that bore this remarkable (if untrue) claim. Rather than issue an expensive recall, the executives let it ride and waited until the next batch to remove the spurious claim. Upon removing mention of the X9 Factor from the bottle, Unilever received slews of complaints from upset customers, claiming that their hair had become less lustrous or that the shampoo was no longer as effective!

Since time immemorial, Wall Street has sold investors a fictional bottle of X9 Factor by means of complicating what is a relatively simple (but not easy) process. As you read Part Two, you may at times find yourself questioning the assumptions within simply because they are too straightforward. Like Dorothy arriving at the end of the Yellow Brick Road, you may be upset to find that there are no Wall Street Wizards, just squatty old men using smoke and mirrors. But just like Dorothy, you may find that letting go of false hope can lead us to a greater reliance on self and a simple focus on doing what matters most.

In the chapters that follow, you will learn a simple approach to consistently doing what has worked in investing. Sounds easy enough, right? Well, it's not. The reason this can be so difficult is that on Wall Street, doing what is "right" can lead to a negative short-term result and doing what is "wrong" can be spectacularly profitable in the short run. Consider the story related by Paul DePodesta, a baseball executive made famous in the book *Moneyball*. He says on his blog, *It Might Be Dangerous*:

> "Many years ago I was playing blackjack in Las Vegas on a Saturday night in a packed casino. I was sitting at third base, and the player who was at first base was playing horribly. He was definitely taking advantage of the free drinks, and it seemed as though every twenty minutes he was dipping into his pocket for more cash.
>
> On one particular hand the player was dealt 17 with his first two cards. The dealer was set to deal the next set of cards and passed right over the player until he stopped her, saying: 'Dealer, I want a hit!' She paused, almost feeling sorry for him, and said, 'Sir, are you sure?' He said yes, and the dealer dealt the card. Sure enough, it was a four.

The place went crazy, high fives all around, everybody hootin' and hollerin', and you know what the dealer said? The dealer looked at the player, and with total sincerity, said: 'Nice hit.'

I thought, 'Nice hit? Maybe it was a nice hit for the casino, but it was a terrible hit for the player! The decision isn't justified just because it worked.' "[82]

My shorthand for the concept illustrated by DePodesta's story is, "you can be right and still be a moron." Perhaps you know a friend who gambled big on a single stock and made a great return. Results notwithstanding, your friend is a moron. Maybe you jumped out of the market right before a precipitous drop because of nothing more than a gut feeling. Lucky you, but you're still a moron.

Exceptional investing over a lifetime cannot be predicated on luck. It must be grounded in a systematic approach that is applied in good times and bad and is never abandoned just because what is popular in the moment may not conform to longer-term best practices.

Just like a casino, if you stick to your discipline in all weather and tilt probability in your favor ever so slightly, you will be greatly rewarded in the end. As Dr. Wes Gray says in *Quantitative Value*, "The power of quantitative investing is in its relentless exploitation of edges."[83] As table 3 of casino odds demonstrates, a small edge, consistently exploited, can produce impressive returns. Casinos don't win by virtue of a huge advantage. They win through good behavior and relentless exploitation of edges. This is the basic premise of RBI.

Table 3—A small edge consistently exploited

Game	House advantage
Roulette (double-zero)	5.3%
Craps (pass/come)	1.4%
Blackjack – average player	2.0%
Blackjack – basic strategy	0.5%
Three Card Poker	3.4%
Slots	5% to 10%
Video Poker	0.5% to 3%

Economist Richard Brealey has said that you would need 25 years of experience with a strategy to determine with 95% accuracy whether or not it had a statistically significant chance of outperformance.[84] Given that 25 years is about the lower end for the investment lifetime of most individuals, it is hard to blame people for chasing returns and doing what has worked most recently (hindsight bias in action) rather than relying on a cohesive investment management system. As Daniel Kahneman says, hindsight bias "leads observers to assess the quality of a decision not by whether the process was sound but whether its outcome was good or bad."[85]

Since you don't have 25 years to burn, you must decide whether a strategy has both intuitive and empirical appeal. I believe that what follows is both philosophically logical and empirically robust. Following the process does not lead to outperformance all of the time, but it is actually the periods of underperformance and the accompanying psychological difficulty that ensure its longer-term appeal. A process that worked every time and required little of those applying it would soon become a crowded trade that loses all efficacy. A system that works over long periods of time, but with shorter periods of psychical pain and underperformance, paradoxically maintains its effectiveness through its imperfection. Like a blackjack player who refuses to hit on 18, doing the right thing pays over time, even if it can be painful to watch the dealer give that three to the person seated next to you.

Before introducing the process, it makes sense to undertake a short State of the Union to determine where money management is at this point in time. In specific, I will examine the strengths and weaknesses of active and passive approaches to investing and propose a model that attempts to build on the strengths of both while minimizing their weaknesses.

The State of Money Management

Passive management: the dangers of playing it safe

PASSIVE INVESTMENT MANAGEMENT is, quite simply, an approach in which a fund's portfolio mirrors a market index (e.g., the S&P 500), or attempts to mirror the performance of an index at least. From a philosophical standpoint, passive management is rooted in a belief in the efficient market hypothesis (EMH). The EMH states that markets quickly and efficiently incorporate all relevant information into prices, making stock-picking an effort in futility.[86] After all, if the price is always right, why bother doing any further research?

Behavioral investors recognize that history tells another story about price dislocations—one that is subtle but meaningful. As Warren Buffett says of Efficient Market Theory (EMT):

"The doctrine (EMT) became highly fashionable—indeed, almost holy scripture in academic circles during the 1970s. Essentially, it said that analyzing stocks was useless because all public information about them was appropriately reflected in their prices. In other words, the market always knew everything. As a corollary, the professors who taught EMT said that someone throwing darts at the stock tables could select a stock portfolio having prospects just as good as one selected by the brightest, most hard-working security analyst. Amazingly, EMT was embraced not only by academics, but also by many investment professionals and corporate managers as well. Observing correctly that the market was frequently efficient, they went on to conclude incorrectly that it was always efficient. The difference between these propositions is night and day."[87]

Since passive management eschews costly research and rock star managers, passive vehicles tend to be far less expensive than their active brethren; a huge win for investors. All else being equal, investors should always choose the least expensive fund as fees cut directly into performance and can dramatically reduce compounding over a lifetime.

The severe negative impact of fees is illustrated in chart 3, where it is assumed an investor saves $500 per month and invests $6000 once per year at an annual return of 6% over 35 years. With no fees (maybe an unrealistic situation, but shown for comparison) the investor's account has grown to $670,000. At annual fees of 1% and 2%, this amount is reduced to $540,000 and $440,000 respectively. The 2% fee represents a staggering $230,000 over 35 years. The message is clear: the lower the fees, the better.

Chart 3—The compounding of fees over a 35-year investment period (6% annual return, $6000 invested per year)

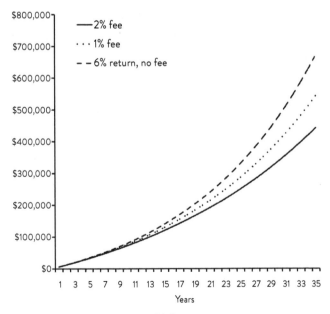

What's more, passive funds are not just inexpensive—they have consistently spanked active funds over just about any timeframe you'd care to consider. Just look at the results of the SPIVA Scorecard, a comparison of how active managers have done relative to their passive counterparts. Over five and ten-year periods respectively, 89% and 82% of large capitalization money managers were beaten by passive approaches to investing (and that's before their fees!). The results for small capitalization stocks, often considered to be less efficiently priced and therefore more favorable to active management, are just as damning: 88% of small cap managers were bested by passive approaches over the past ten years.[88]

With miniscule fees and impressive returns, it's no wonder that investors from Warren Buffett on down recommend passive vehicles as the best choice for most retail investors. But are there weaknesses to this sensible approach? Yup, there are.

A faulty framework

Just as an architectural structure is only as sound as the foundation upon which it is built, an approach to investing can be no better than the ideas that undergird it. That foundation, in the case of the efficient market hypothesis, is shaky at best.

The central notion of EMH, that "the price is always right" has proven laughably false over the course of recorded financial history. Over 400 years ago, in what is one of the first recorded bubbles in financial history, a single commodity traded for ten times the annual salary of a skilled laborer. Records from that time show that this commodity was traded in some cases for as much as 12 acres of prime farmland and even swapped directly for single-family dwellings.

What was this precious commodity, you ask? A single tulip bulb. During what we now refer to as Tulip Mania, the Dutch became convinced that the price of tulips would never fall because of their singular nature and bid the prices up accordingly. In the event that you can find an obtuse economist willing to argue that "the price is always right", you should immediately concede on the condition that they will gift you their house in exchange for a single tulip bulb.

But prices becoming grossly disconnected from fundamental value is not some ancient construct which Modern Man has outgrown. As recently as 1998, eToys.com, an internet start-up company, had a total market capitalization of $8 billion on sales of $30 million and profits of −$28.6 million. Its closest competitor, the "stodgy" veteran Toys"R"Us, had sales more than 40 times greater, and was profitable, but had only three-quarters the market capitalization.[89]

The reason for this huge discrepancy was investor enthusiasm over the then-new internet. Of course, Toys"R"Us had a website for selling toys as well, but manic investors were unable to see past the seemingly unlimited profits promised by the new batch of online start-ups. In this euphoric state, traditional metrics like sales and profitability were ignored in favor of vague hopes; only for those hopes to be dashed on the rocks of cold economic realities. eToys went bankrupt toward the end of the tech bubble, only to be acquired by—you guessed it—Toys"R"Us in 2009.

Inasmuch as one of the foundational assumptions of EMH is demonstrably false, it stands to reason that an investment discipline built upon this assumption can be improved upon. Jim Grant said it far more interestingly: "To suppose that the value of a stock is determined purely by earnings is to forget that people have burned witches."

Passive in name only

To listen to some of the most devoted adherents of passive management, one might assume that the indexes tracked by these investors were the product of some inviolable process. The dirty little secret of a passive index like the S&P 500 is that it's not, well, passive at all. The stated mandate of the Standard and Poor's methodology is to choose a basket of stocks that reflects the broader US economy by including "leading companies in leading industries." Arnott describes their methods in his book *The Fundamental Index*:

"The process is subjective—not entirely rules based and certainly not formulaic. There are many who argue that the S&P 500 isn't an index at all: It's an actively managed portfolio selected by a committee—whose very membership is a closely guarded secret!—and has shown a stark growth bias throughout its recent history of additions and deletions.... The result is that the Standard and Poor's is predisposed to add 'popular' stocks and those that have performed well recently, rather than those with potential to improve on recent poor results."[90]

Simply put, financial indices are a product of active human intervention and, as such, are prone to all of the biases that beset regular investors.

To illustrate the damaging effects of this subjectivity, Arnott discusses some of the changes made to the index in recent years. In 1995, 33 additions were made to the S&P 500, with a scant four of these additions being drawn from the tech-heavy NASDAQ index. In 2000, however, at the height of the tech craze, 24 of the 58 companies added to the S&P 500 were tech issues from the NASDAQ. In addition, the committee bypassed what few bylaws it did have for inclusion to allow for the addition of popular but unprofitable companies like AOL. By ignoring their sensible rules, the S&P 500 committee actively loaded the boat on their "passive" index just in time for catastrophic losses in the tech stocks they had just added.

The result of this hubris on the part of the committee seriously damaged everyday investors. From March 2000 to March 2002, the average stock gained 20% while the now-tech-heavy S&P lost 20%. A secretly appointed committee adding stocks to a portfolio with few governing rules does not look much different in practice than a mutual fund manager making additions based on similarly loose logic. For this reason, passive investment vehicles may not be as passive as you'd imagined and may subject you to all of the same return-chasing behavior present in nominally active approaches.

A behavioral glitch

Ask anyone on the street the one thing that they know about investing and they are likely to blithely say, "Buy low, sell high." The primary problem with passive investing is that it systematically violates this very first rule. The indices that passive vehicles track are very often capitalization weighted, meaning that the larger the total value of a company's stock, the larger a portion of the index they represent. As Rob Arnott says, "the capitalization-weighted implementation of the index fund concept is flawed. Because the size of our investment in any company is linked to stock prices, the capitalization-weighted portfolio overweights the overvalued stocks and underweights the undervalued stocks."

It is just as stocks get more expensive, and thus less attractive to buy, that their power within a cap-weighted index grows. Simultaneously, stocks that have been beaten down and may present excellent buying opportunities have diminished power. In a very real sense, index investing locks in the exact opposite of what we ought to be doing and causes us to buy high and sell low.

Index investing, widely considered to be the sensible approach for retail investors, has at its nucleus a damaging behavioral cancer. Buying a capitalization weighted index like the S&P 500 means that you would have held nearly 50% tech stocks in 2000 and nearly 40% financials in 2008. Just as surely as indexing combats some behavioral tendencies like underdiversification and overpaying, it makes others law. A behavioral approach to investing must hold on to the best of indexing, and there is much to emulate, but must also improve upon its tendency to load the boat with large, expensive stocks, which are historically some of the worst performers of all.

Everyone on the same
side of the boat

I am writing this book at the end of 2019, a year in which assets invested in US passive funds exceeded actively-managed assets for the first time.[91] It appears as if passive is winning.

But if there is one lesson to be learned from financial history, it is that universal consensus tends to portend bad news. As Aaron Task said in his thoughtful blog piece, 'Pride Cometh Before the Fall: Indexing Edition', "when 'everybody' knows something, it's usually a good time to head in the opposite direction. And what 'everybody' knows now is that the very best, smartest investment you can make is an index fund."[92]

Jesse Felder, another intelligent voice warning of the dangers of indexing has said, " 'passive investing' will ultimately become a victim of its own success. The massive shift to index funds over the past 15 years or so drove the valuations of the largest index components to levels which guarantee poor returns going forward. Poor returns, in turn, will guarantee these inflows will turn to outflows and the virtuous cycle will become a vicious one."[93] As Nassim Taleb says, "We have been fragilizing the economy, our health, political life, education, almost everything… by suppressing randomness and volatility… This is the tragedy of modernity: as with neurotically overprotective parents, those trying to help are often hurting us the most."[94] In capital markets, the right thing to do ceases to be the right thing to do when everyone does it.

Index funds perform because they are appropriately diversified and low cost, but they also leave valuable returns on the table by failing to exploit some of what we know about "what works." As Warren Buffett says of EMH approaches to investing like indexing, "What could be more advantageous in an intellectual contest—whether it be chess, bridge, or stock selection than to have opponents who have been taught that thinking is a waste of energy."

With just a tiny bit more thought and application, average investors can apply the lessons of history to improve returns, all while avoiding the tendency of indexing to overweight the most bloated and expensive companies available. The evidence is unavoidable that passive indexing is a good approach to investing, but by eliminating its systematic behavioral bias we can do much better still.

The unfulfilled promise of active investing

If index investing is designed to mirror a market benchmark, active investing can simply be thought of as an investment style that seeks to outperform a representative market benchmark. The ostensible benefit of an active approach is that it has the potential to both outperform and manage risk, but while some active managers have lived up to this dual mandate, many have not. Much like smoking or eating processed meat, actively managing money has experienced a reputational decline over the last 25 or so years. While some of this is unfair (endless hand-wringing about high frequency trading), active management has done much to earn its bad reputation.

The damning truth about active management is that it's a zero sum game before fees, meaning that active efforts are reductive on average. Just as the average record of every Major League Baseball team will always be .500, the average performance of active managers will always be, well, average—and that's before the fees. This line of reasoning is often heard from detractors of active management, who will smugly assert, "It's just math."

But as Rob Arnott says, "The fact that active managers haven't been able to exploit pricing errors for above-benchmark performance does not provide any evidence that those errors are small, because the average results of the average active manager are a foregone conclusion."[95] Just as the collective mediocrity of baseball teams doesn't make watching baseball any less enjoyable—and after all one team will win the World Series every year—so too mustn't the collective mediocrity of asset managers be the only reason we choose to invest in a particular way. The structural difficulties of outperformance say everything about the group but nothing about any manager in particular—a good thing to keep in mind the next time you hear, "It's just math."

The asset manager attempting to achieve outsized performance begins with a significant handicap in the form of trading fees and management costs. After all, Harvard PhDs in financial engineering don't work for free! As cited in *The Fundamental Index*, the impact of these two obstacles is dramatic, accounting for between 0.5% and 2% annual underperformance for active managers. A mere 2% may not sound like much, but realize that an investment of $100,000 that compounds at 10% a year will grow to $1.74 million over 30 years, whereas that same investment compounded minus 2% fees grows to just $1 million over that same timeframe.

Another source of disruption is that many active managers close up shop every year and may not be reported in performance figures. A study by Arnott, Berkin and Ye shows that when the failed funds are included in performance figures, the underperformance of active funds may be as dramatic as 2% to 4% per year.[96] To revisit our example, a return of 6% a year (our 10% return, less 4% underperformance per year) yields a mere $574,000—quite a price to pay! The behavioral investor understands the corrosive power of fees and trading costs and must seek to minimize both wherever possible.

Few investors would begrudge active managers their paycheck if they showed evidence of discipline and skill, but the research suggests that professionals are just as prone to making boneheaded mistakes as you or I. Charles Ellis points out in *The Elements of Investing*, "professionally managed funds tend to have their lowest cash positions at market tops and highest cash positions at market bottoms."[97] Just like us, they greedily load up when stocks are expensive and sell in panic when stocks become attractively priced. Thanks for nothing, money managers.

What's more, the research even suggests that it is difficult to choose which money managers will do well. Dr. Brian Portnoy cites evidence that only 5% of professional fund of fund managers show discernible skill at their jobs.[98] If people who are paid handsomely to select winning money managers are unable to do so, what chance in Hell do you have of doing likewise? The lessons for behavioral investors are unavoidable: you must automate your process wherever possible and avoid bias in the selection of people and processes. To do otherwise is to believe that professional money managers are actually above the fray of human bias, when the evidence shows us otherwise.

Active managers have of late been quick to scapegoat the broader environment—accommodative Fed policies, recovering from the throes of a deep recession—but the fact is that the trends discussed above are pervasive and long-standing. As Jason Zweig of the *Wall Street Journal* says:

"Despite what you've heard and what many of you fervently believe, underperformance is not merely a temporary by-product of the narrow market of the past few years. Over the decade ended in mid-1974, 89% of all money managers lagged the S&P 500. Over the 20 years ended in 1964, the average fund underperformed by roughly 110 basis points. Even from 1929 through 1950, not a single major mutual fund beat the S&P. Take any period you like; the results are invariably discouraging."[99]

I am encouraged by the fact that a number of prominent active money managers are integrating the findings of behavioral finance into their processes. Brinker Capital, UBS, BlackRock, Barclays, Merrill Lynch, Allianz, J.P. Morgan and many more brokerage firms and asset managers are creating entire teams of behavioral experts to improve their trading and the delivery of advice. Although there are pockets of progress, many active money managers have not done their job for some time now, and their failings stem largely from an unawareness of their own flawed humanity. They have overtraded, charged excessive fees, fallen prey to emotional traps and, as we will discuss later, not differentiated themselves meaningfully from passive approaches.

I believe in the potential of active management to both exploit behavioral mispricing and protect investors from catastrophic loss, but realizing this potential hinges on a deep understanding of investment psychology. If active management is to flourish, it must do so on its potential merits—risk management, performance, accounting for behavioral bias—and not on false promises.

As a result of the trends discussed over the last few pages, the investment industry is becoming increasingly divided between advocates of what have traditionally been considered active and passive investing. But as we have discussed the two approaches, you will have seen that both have their strengths and weaknesses. Active management provides the hope of outsized performance and managed risk, whereas indexing has lower fees and tends to have lower turnover. Inasmuch as all investing is active, indexing included (aside from true global capitalization weighting), it makes more sense to discuss what works and what doesn't, relentlessly exploiting every edge at our disposal, rather than engage in semantic bickering.

Investment vehicles that perform have tended to have the following characteristics: diversified, low turnover, low fee and allowance made for behavioral bias. Investing that doesn't work is just the opposite: expensive, undiversified, frequently traded and failure to account for bad behavior. By blending the best parts and removing the worst parts of these two schools of thought, we can achieve a moderately priced option that accounts for investor behavior, minimizes transaction costs and seeks to outperform the broad market.

Table 4 summarises how this RBI approach combines the most desirable parts of both active and passive investment management.

Table 4—Rule-based behavioral investing

	Low fee	Diversified	Potential outperformance	Low turnover	Manages bias
RBI	✓	✓	✓	✓	✓
Passive	✓	✓		✓	
Active		✓	✓		

Managing
Behavioral Risk

AS YOU'VE NOW seen, the conversation around asset management has historically involved the false dichotomy of active versus passive. This is a conversation that is intensely meaningful to Wall Street salespeople, but helps investors very little.

Once we realize that passive indexes are not mined from the Earth, but rather assembled arbitrarily by committee, the most pertinent question is not if you are actively investing (you are) but how best to actively invest. If you are destined to be active, you might as well be good at it! But before we answer the question, "How can I become a skilled active investment manager?" we must first answer the less-sexy-but-more-important question, "How can I not suck at being an active investment manager?"

Just as good defense wins championships but the quarterback gets the girl, risk management drives performance but big returns get all of the press. If you accept this as fact and pick up a textbook on risk management, you are likely to read about two primary types of investment risk—systematic and unsystematic.

Systematic risk, also known as "market risk", is the chance you will lose money as a result of moves in the broad market as opposed to any business in particular. Diversification does not provide any real protection against systematic risk because a sinking tide lowers all boats and it includes "acts of God" like natural disasters. Unsystematic risk, also referred to as "business risk", is the chance that an investment in an individual security will depreciate in value. This type of risk can and ought to be hedged against through diversification—a topic that we will cover in some depth later.

What your textbook will likely omit altogether is a third type of risk—behavioral risk—that is at least as important as its better-known brethren. Behavioral risk is the potential for your actions to increase the probability of permanent loss of capital. Systematic risk is a failure of markets, unsystematic risk is a failure of business and behavioral risk is a failure of self.

Although most classically trained investors would not articulate behavioral risk as one of the primary investment risk factors (schooled as they are in traditional ideas about the duality of risk), they are agreeable enough to its inclusion once the subject has been broached. We can all easily think of instances when our faulty thinking led to disastrous consequences (Why did I think that shooting my bow and arrow at the pool cover was a good idea?).

But if general acceptance is a given, codification of such a nebulous construct is a much different conversation. This is something we need to achieve, since defining a universe of behavioral risk is a prerequisite to its management. After all, how can you fight a monster you can't see? Once we have this definition, our model of behavioral risk will then give rise to an investment philosophy that is robust to bad decisions, after which we can discuss the specifics of security selection. It all starts with risk, as illustrated in the following flow diagram.

Figure 2—Behavioral risk flow diagram

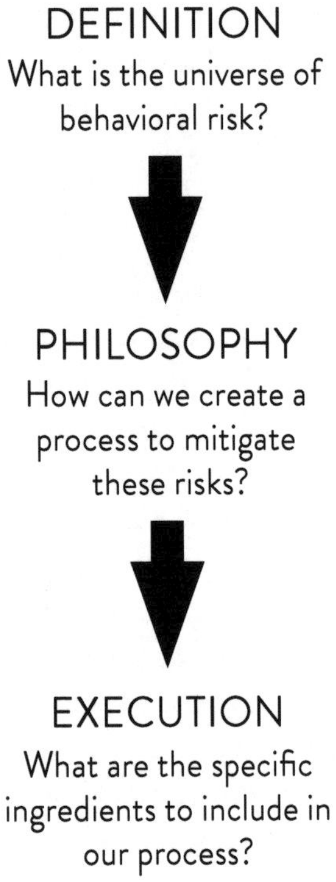

DEFINITION
What is the universe of
behavioral risk?

PHILOSOPHY
How can we create a
process to mitigate
these risks?

EXECUTION
What are the specific
ingredients to include in
our process?

To begin to get a handle on the multitudinous ways in which we can screw up a portfolio with our faulty logic, we begin by engaging in something psychologists call "catastrophizing". Much like "funner", "catastrophizing" isn't really a word but it ought to be. Catastrophizing is the act by which you let your mind run wild to think of every possible negative outcome. A typical example looks something like this:

I begin with a worry that I might have done poorly on my Algebra test. Simple enough, but it spirals quickly from there. "Oh no," I fantasize, "if I didn't do well on my Algebra test, I'm not going to get into Stanford. If I don't get into Stanford, my parents will be ashamed of me. If I don't get into Stanford AND my parents hate me, I'll have to live in the basement, attend Diploma Mill Community College and endure awkward dinners with my folks every night. The stress will cause me to overeat, which will cause me to develop acne, which means that I'll never go on another date. This pattern will continue until I die a 55-year-old virgin whose morbidly obese corpse will have to be extracted from the basement via forklift." And to think, it's all been set in motion by the Algebra test.

That, my friends, is an A+ catastrophizing session! Typically this kind of thinking is maladaptive, causing us to inflate the likelihood of negative events and overlook the myriad resources at our disposal. But in the case of trying to stress test a universe of behavioral risk, it might just do the trick.

Misbehaving, Richard Thaler's incredible origin story of the field of behavioral economics, recounts the simple but effective way that he set the field on its current course. Incredulous about what he was learning about efficient markets, Thaler set out to brainstorm all of the real-life ways in which the people he knew differed from the "Econs" (i.e., fictional individuals who optimize utility and always make rational financial decisions) he was learning about in his theory courses. Using nothing more than a simple thought experiment, Thaler created the list of anomalies that launched a thousand research projects and vastly deepened our understanding of how mere mortals make financial decisions.

While the discovery and documentation of these behavioral anomalies was an important first step, they lack utility to investors inasmuch as there is no broader organizing framework. We now have long lists of the ways in which we are imperfect, but little in the way of practical next steps. As we learned from the example of the Thai prisoner release, bad news without a concrete solution set can actually exacerbate the problem!

Inspired by the simple elegance of Thaler's approach, I put on my catastrophic thinking cap and set out to brainstorm every possible way someone's behavior could negatively impact investment decision-making. I generated almost 40 ways. From there, I looked for common psychological underpinnings among the various modes of mismanagement in an effort to group these mistakes into common units amenable to treatment. I began this process without preconceptions of how the information would shake out. Five consistent types of behavioral risk emerged:

1. Ego
2. Emotion
3. Information
4. Attention
5. Conservation

The number of bad decisions we can make is limitless (have you seen reality TV?), but all behavioral risk has one or more of these five risk factors at its core. This classification is unique to this book and provides an important starting point for the creation of behaviourally-informed investment management processes. If we can understand and combat each of these behavioral risks through our investing process, we are on the way to removing behavioral risk from our investing.

Figure 3 illustrates the five dimensions of behavioral risk. Following the diagram, I explore each of the five types in more detail.

Figure 3—The five dimensions of behavioral risk

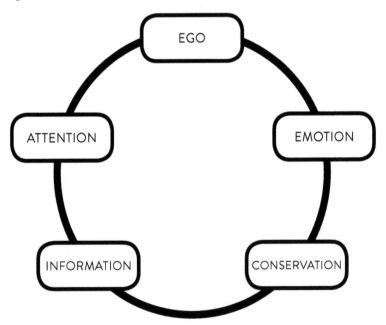

1. Ego risk

Ego risk is made manifest in behaviors that privilege our need for felt personal competency at the expense of clear-eyed decision making. Specific examples might include good old-fashioned overconfidence, a tendency to become defensive when pet ideas are challenged (backfire effect), or a belief that one's mere involvement in a project makes it more likely to succeed (the awesomely named IKEA effect).

Ego risk leaves specific evidence of its presence in overly concentrated positions, churning and the use of excessive leverage. Whatever the specific manifestation, the source is always the same—an ego that privileges its own care and feeding over making good decisions.

Examples of ego risk

- **Choice supportive bias**—the tendency to ascribe positive attributes to a chosen investment decision and denigrate the road not taken.
- **Overconfidence**—felt competency or knowledge that exceeds actual competency or knowledge.
- **Confirmation bias**—the propensity to seek out information that confirms an investment thesis and ignore disconfirmatory information.
- **Endowment effect**—the tendency to perceive a stock as valuable simply because we own it.
- **Semmelweis reflex**—the reflexive rejection of information that disagrees with a cherished idea or opinion.
- **Illusion of control**—proneness to believe we are more in charge of market outcomes than is truly the case.
- **False consensus**—overestimating the degree to which others agree with our investment ideas.

2. Information risk

Information risk is realized when incomplete, flawed or misweighted data gives rise to decisions that are equally defective. Certainly there can be factual mistakes in the information on which we base our decisions, but our focus here is the ways in which the human mind can contort even the cleanest data set. Given that data in abstraction are meaningless, the information we possess is only as "clean" as the process by which it is considered.

Information risk shows itself through our ignorance of probability (base rate fallacy), our mistaken notion that more information is always better and, most damningly, through our unawareness of our own biases. In portfolio management it shows itself in misunderstanding the complexity or liquidity of our positions, focusing on outcomes over process and failing to distinguish signal from noise when considering all sides of an investment thesis. Wall Street spends countless millions each year improving the speed at which information is delivered and securing proprietary signals. This is all well and good, but the behavioral investor understands information is only as good as the person tasked with making sense of it.

Examples of information risk

- **Base rate fallacy**—penchant for ignoring probability in favor of specific information that may be more eye-catching.
- **Blind spot bias**—the ability to recognize flawed thinking in others but not ourselves; "unknown unknowns" in Donald-Rumsfeld-speak.
- **Information bias**—the mistaken belief that more information, no matter how trivial, is always better when making an investment decision.
- **Ambiguity aversion**—the preference for known risk over unknown risk.

- **Conservatism**—the slow incorporation of new information based on a mistaken belief that the future will look much like the recent past.
- **Triviality**—the inclination to give significant weight to insignificant information.
- **Normalcy bias**—the underestimation of a market crash and its potential effects.

3. Emotion Risk

Emotion risk stems from the fact that our perceptions of risk are colored by both our transitory emotional states and our individual propensity toward positivity or negativity. Emotion leads most of us to underrate the possibility of bad things happening to us (optimism bias), to avoid even thinking about what might go wrong (ostrich effect) and to ignore the important role emotion plays in our decisions (empathy gap). When fear does break through, it can become so powerful that we can be immobilized by trying to avoid pain (negativity bias).

Investors looking for examples of emotion bias in their decision-making should begin with periods of market turbulence. Examine trades for risk taking or safety seeking during periods of elevated sentiment. Also, look for herd following (fearful when others are fearful) versus appropriate contrarianism (greedy when others are fearful) at historical market tops and bottoms.

Research has shown that emotion plays an important role in facilitating choice. In fact, people with damage to certain parts of their brain that process emotion are rendered unable to make even everyday decisions such as what to wear. The key is not to be free of emotion altogether, but to understand our personal susceptibilities to stress, panic and fear of missing out.

Examples of emotion risk

- **Affect heuristic**—the tendency for current emotional state to color risk perception.
- **Empathy gap**—underestimating our reliance on emotion and overestimating our use of logic when making decisions.
- **Negativity effect**—bias toward negative events and thoughts impacting our risk-perception much more powerfully than positive events.
- **Optimism bias**—mistaken belief that we are less likely to experience a negative event than others.
- **Ostrich effect**—attempting to avoid risk by pretending it does not exist.
- **Risk compensation**—tendency to adjust risk-taking behavior relative to subjective experience of risk (accounts for drivers going faster when wearing a seatbelt).
- **Restraint bias**—fallacious belief in our ability to control our own impulses in the face of intense emotion.

4. Attention risk

Attention risk is born of our disposition to evaluate information in relative terms and let salience trump probability when making investment decisions. "Salience" is the psychological term for prominence, meaning that our attention can be hijacked by low-probability-high-scariness things like shark attacks while ignoring high-probability-low-scariness dangers like eating at Taco Bell. We also tend to rate the unfamiliar as more risky and show a preference for domestic stocks (home bias) and familiar names (mere exposure effect), regardless of their fundamental qualities.

Those looking for concrete evidence of attention risk in their investing should be on the lookout for crowded trades, overreliance on domestic stocks, excessive correlation and high-noise-low-probability investments based on a collective moment of panic (e.g., the Ebola scare). Dr. Bob Nease suggests that of the ten million bits of information our brains process each second, a mere 50 bits are allotted to conscious thought! When so much of what pulls our thoughts and actions happens below the surface, we must be very intentional with how we spend the little attention that is within our power.

Examples of attention risk

- **Anchoring**—penchant to rely too heavily on the first piece of information (e.g., price paid for a stock) when making investment decisions.
- **Availability bias**—confusing the ease of recalling information with its impact or probability.
- **Attention bias**—proneness to confuse our own rumination on a subject with its actual importance.
- **Home bias**—bias toward viewing domestic equities as more safe and knowable than their international counterparts.
- **Framing effect**—the tendency for our perception of risk to vary depending on whether it is framed as a loss or a gain.
- **Mere exposure effect**—phenomenon by which we view stocks as less risky if we are familiar with the company.

5. Conservation risk

Conservation risk is a by-product of our asymmetrical preference for gain relative to loss and the status quo relative to change. We like winning much more than losing and the old way much better than the new way, all of which contorts our ability to see the world clearly. This conservation effect can be observed in our resistance to new ways of being (status quo bias), our preference for no risk at all relative to large incremental decreases in risk (zero risk bias) and an aptness to privilege our current self over the needs of our future self (hyperbolic discounting).

Evidence of selling winning stocks too quickly and holding losing stocks too long, a failure to maintain appropriate risk levels when "up" and signs of taking excessive risks when "down" are all good signs that you might have fallen prey to conservation risk. Our aversion to change and loss are primal and can only be unseated by a deliberate process aimed at recognizing and overcoming our behavioral inertia.

Examples of conservation risk

- **Loss aversion**—the asymmetrical relationship between gain and loss, whereby losses sting far worse than gains feel good.
- **Status quo bias**—human preference for things to remain as they are.
- **Sunk cost fallacy**—reasoning that further risk must be taken in an attempt to recoup past losses.
- **Normalcy bias**—the belief that all that has been is all that will ever be.
- **Zero risk bias**—preference for the total elimination of specific risks, even when alternative choices offer a greater overall reduction in risk.
- **Disposition effect**—behavioral tendency to sell stocks that have appreciated and to hold stocks that have fallen in value.
- **Hyperbolic discounting**—tendency to dramatically discount rewards that occur in the future relative to those occurring in the present.

Solving with a simple process

Let's take a moment to review what we now know before determining what to do with all of this great information. We know that the active versus passive conversation is outdated and that instead we should focus on what works versus what does not in investing. We know that what works are strategies that are diversified, low-fee, low-turnover, and account for behavioral biases. We further understand that traditional notions of risk are not the only dangers we face and that our own behavior poses at least as great a threat as business or market risks. Specifically, we must design a process that is resistant to emotion, ego, bad information, misplaced attention and our natural tendency to be loss averse. No small task, but reflecting on what we know about the River Jordan, we understand that complex problems can have simple but elegant solutions.

One way to combat the ill effects of behavioral risk is to create individual interventions aimed at its five facets. For instance, we might confront ego risk by taking a sweeping personal inventory of our own successes and failures, trying to arrive at a more nuanced understanding of our own strengths and weaknesses. Likewise, we might manage emotion risk by ensuring that we are getting proper exercise and not consuming too much caffeine, both of which would help to regulate our emotions. Such discretionary efforts are laudable and appeal to common sense, but ultimately aren't enough. Restraint bias tells us that we can be strong in the face of fear, but experience and research alike tell us that willpower and personal dedication are almost never enough. A far more reliable way to combat behavioral risk is to create a simple process that accounts for each of the five facets and to follow that process unfailingly.

The myriad behavioral traps to which we can fall prey can largely be mitigated through the simple but elegant process that is RBI. The process is easily remembered by the following four Cs:

1. **Consistency**—frees us from the pull of ego, emotion and loss aversion, while focusing our efforts on uniform execution.
2. **Clarity**—we prioritize evidence-based factors and are not pulled down the seductive path of worrying about the frightening but unlikely or the exciting but useless.
3. **Courageousness**—we automate the process of contrarianism: doing what the brain knows to be best but the heart and stomach have trouble accomplishing.
4. **Conviction**—helps us walk the line between hubris and fear by creating portfolios that are diverse enough to be humble and focused enough to offer a shot at long-term outperformance.

To deepen our understanding of how RBI can manage behavioral risk, let's explore each of the four Cs in greater detail.

The Four Cs of Rule-Based Behavioral Investing

To recap, the four Cs of rule-based behavioral investing—which can help us to defeat behavioural risk—are as follows:

1. Consistency
2. Clarity
3. Courageousness
4. Conviction

Let's delve into these in more detail.

1. Consistency

"Consistency is the last refuge of the unimaginative."

—**Oscar Wilde**

Warning: I am about to give you some news that will be hard for you to accept. Are you ready? Here it is—a simple formula is better than you at selecting investments. What's that you say, you went to an Ivy League school? A simple formula is better than you at selecting investments. Ah, you're a CFA? A simple formula is better than you at selecting investments.

As a human family, we hate hearing that our genius can be outsourced or that—gasp—we can be bested by a machine! After all, who didn't cheer for Kasparov versus Deep Blue or Rocky against Ivan Drago? Hearing that a process beats a person is simply inconsistent with our romantic notions about the nobility of humankind, but alas, it's demonstrably true in investment management.

Ideas about mankind's greatness are understandable and rooted in a belief in personal excellence and free will. But evidence from the world of marketing shows us just how contextual our behaviors really are. Martin Lindstrom reports that, "when classical music was piped over loudspeakers in the London Underground, robberies dropped by 33%, assaults on staff by 25%, and vandalism of trains and stations by 37%."[100]

He goes on to relate that environment can determine whether we choose to buy a bottle of French Chardonnay or German Riesling. Says Lindstrom, "Over a two-week period, two researchers at the University of Leicester played either accordion heavy, recognizably French music or a German bierkeller brass band over the speakers of the wine section inside a large supermarket. On French music days, 77% of consumers bought French wine, whereas on bierkeller music days, the vast majority of consumers made a beeline for the German section of the store."

If something as simple as music can impact everything from vandalism to vino, imagine how dramatically our behavior is shaped by the bombardment of financial news and opinions we receive during a time of financial tumult. An investor may know in her heart that she ought to be greedy when others are fearful, but she is also receiving powerful contextual cues in the form of CNBC commentators telling her that the sky is falling, to say nothing of the fear she feels when opening her quarterly portfolio statements. In the absence of decisional constraints imposed by a strict process, it is easy to see how investors can make the wrong buy and sell decisions!

The limits of common sense

One reason why we are loath to accept that a process can outperform our intuition is that in many cases, our intuition works nicely, thank you very much. You understand intuitively that if you are cooking and pulling something out of the stove, it would be wise of you to wear hot pads on your hands. This is an example of a simple process that provides immediate feedback ("OUCH! $%#@*!") and is performed with regularity.

Investing is a special case as it is the exact opposite—a process that is performed infrequently, provides delayed feedback and includes an overwhelmingly complex array of variables. Nobel laureate Daniel Kahneman created a list of five variables that lead to suboptimal decision-making and it could not describe stock picking more perfectly. They are:

1. A complex problem
2. Incomplete and changing information
3. Changing and competing goals
4. High stress, high stakes involved
5. The need to interact with others to make decisions

Unlike run-of-the-mill decisions that common sense handles nicely, investing lends itself to process over intuition by virtue of the number, complexity and dynamism of variables involved. All of our decisions are influenced by something: decision-making abhors a vacuum as much as nature ever did. Rule-based decision-making just ensures that we are focused on the right thing rather than peripheral variables that distract from the true mission. You don't need a checklist to take that casserole out of the oven, but you're awfully glad that your airplane pilot uses one and you should expect no less from the person managing your money (whether that's you or a professional).

Despite Emerson's belief that "a foolish consistency is the hobgoblin of little minds," great people from all walks of life have embraced the paradoxical freedom of a formula. US President Barack Obama limited his clothing choices to ensure that his mind was free to focus on the weightier matters of governing. Nick Saban, arguably the best college football coach of all time, has the same thing for breakfast (two Little Debbie oatmeal cream pies!) and lunch (salad) every day, to minimize distractions and fully focus on coaching. Both men either implicitly or explicitly understand what the research on "decisional fatigue" has taught us—that exercising restraint or expending energy to make one decision respectively frees up or robs us of the reserves to do the same on our next decision.

A father who spends an hour at the grocery store agonizing over price-per-ounce is likely to squander his savings in a fit of exhaustion by making an impulse purchase while checking out. A person on a diet may cave to an outrageous binge after a week's worth of self-denial. Our capacity for intense focus and restraint are limited and today's moderation sows the seeds for tomorrow's excess, unless we automate the process by which we make decisions altogether.

The applications to investing are obvious. It is torturous to be conservative in the face of market mania or to snatch up bargains in the throes of a panic. So torturous that making and remaking that decision every day would break even the toughest investor, unless she has a discipline that she follows with exactness. As Jim Simons says of this process, "… if you're going to trade using models, you should just slavishly use the models. You do whatever the hell it says no matter how smart or dumb you think it is now."

Physician, heal thyself

I've tried to make the philosophical case for rule-based decisions, but perhaps you still want to believe in the triumph of human ingenuity over automation (hard to blame you!). If so, I hope that an appeal to the research will change your mind.

Joel Greenblatt is a billionaire hedge fund manager and author of some of the most accessible writing on value investing. Greenblatt's most popular book, *The Little Book That Still Beats the Market*, introduced what he refers to as his "Magic Formula"—a system for combining value considerations with return on invested capital to create portfolios.

Capitalizing on the popularity (and impressive track record) of his Magic Formula, Greenblatt offered investors two options: they could invest with his firm through a managed account or could exercise discretion by removing Magic Formula stocks they found unattractive. The managed account option followed the Magic Formula with exactness—it blindly bought the stocks that scored highest on combined measures of value and return. The discretionary condition allowed investors to use their judgment, screening out stocks they thought would be bad investments, and doing further fundamental research.

Over the course of the two years of Greenblatt's study, the automated Magic Formula accounts returned 84.1%, significantly besting the index (S&P 500) return of 62.7% over that same time period. The discretionary accounts, on the other hand, underperformed the benchmark, returning just 59.4%. By using their own discretion, investors systematically and reliably excluded the best-performing stocks, likely because they looked scary at the time of purchase. In an effort to outperform a powerful model, human effort led to worse outcomes than doing nothing at all!

Retail investors are not the only ones who ignore rule-based frameworks to their own detriment; this very human tendency extends to some of Wall Street's best and brightest. The September 16, 2004 issue of *The Wall Street Journal* featured an exposé on Value Line, a vaunted research firm with an unrivaled history of picking great stocks in their research reports. Value Line also has a mutual fund that one would presume would benefit from being housed within an organization famed for its research.

Over the five-year period examined, the Value Line mutual fund returned a cumulative negative 19%, while investors following the advice in the Value Line research reports gained an impressive 76%! The discrepancy? The managers of the Value Line fund did not rely on their own company's research to make decisions, presumably supposing that they knew better themselves. Behavioral investor James Montier was really on to something when he said, "As much as we all like to think we can add something to the quant model output, the truth is that very often quant models represent a ceiling in performance (from which we detract) rather than a floor (to which we can add)."[101]

A 1968 study by Lewis Goldberg analyzed the performance of a model-based approach to assessing mental illness versus the clinical judgment of trained doctors. Not only did the simple model outperform the psychologists head-to-head, but it also bested psychologists who were given access to the model.[102]

Models have also been shown to outperform human judgment in predicting the outcomes of Supreme Court decisions,[103] Presidential elections,[104] movie preferences,[105] prison recidivism, wine quality, marital satisfaction and military success, to name just a few of the over 45 domains in which they have demonstrated their superiority.[106] A meta-analysis performed by William Grove, David Zald, Boyd Lebow, Beth Snitz and Chad Nelson found that models equal or beat expert decision-making a whopping 94.12% of the time, meaning that they are only defeated by human discretion 5.88% of the time.[107]

Forecasting guru Philip Tetlock says emphatically what the meta-analysis says statistically: "It is impossible to find any domain in which humans clearly outperformed crude extrapolation algorithms, less still sophisticated statistical ones."[108] The research is unequivocal—if you are using human judgment instead of a process to make investment decisions, you are doing more work for a diminished result.

Flirting with models

The reaction to the evidence discussed above is undeniably unsettling; it eats at the very core of what it means to be human. Two common responses to this sort of cognitive dissonance are, "Can we combine judgment and models to get the best of both?" and "We need more education to improve human judgment!"

Sadly, both approaches are flawed. If you'll recall the above, there were a number of instances cited in which judgment was combined with models. While this quantamental (quantitative + fundamental) approach has some intuitive appeal, the results tend to be better than judgment alone but worse than the model alone. A big part of this human underperformance is our tendency to misweigh the importance of one variable versus another. As Nassim Taleb says of this combinatorial approach:

"We are faulty and there is no need to bother trying to correct our flaws. We are so defective and so mismatched to our environment that we can't just work around these flaws. I am convinced of that after spending almost all of my adult and professional years in a fierce fight between my brain and my emotions in which the only success I've had is in going around my emotions rather than rationalizing them. Perhaps ridding ourselves of our humanity is not in the works; we need wily tricks, not some grandiose moralizing help. As an empiricist (actually a skeptical empiricist) I despise the moralizers beyond anything on this planet: I wonder why they blindly believe in ineffectual methods. Delivering advice assumes that our cognitive apparatus rather than our emotional machinery exerts some meaningful control over our actions... modern behavioral science shows this to be completely untrue."[109]

The educational angle—trying to improve human judgment through learning—also has intuitive appeal, since we rightly value education and see its power in other parts of our lives. The sad truth about education with respect to decision-making under duress is that it is most wanting when it is most needed! Studies suggest that we lose roughly 13% of our cognitive capacity under stress, meaning that even if we are schooled in what we ought to do, our emotions override our lessons. Once again, Taleb is wise: "Even once we are aware of our biases, we must recognize that knowledge does not equal behavior. The solution lies in designing and adopting an investment process that is at least partially robust to behavioral decision-making errors."

As further evidence, Dinkelman, Levinsohn and Majelantle show that 91% of men in Botswana said they knew the use of a condom would help prevent AIDS/HIV, yet only 70% use one. 92% of women knew condoms worked but only 63% used them.[110] A little closer to home, you don't overeat, yell at your kids or fail to exercise because of a lack of knowledge, you do so because emotions override reason in that moment. Education, it would seem, is no substitute for behavioral guardrails. Imagine how healthy you would be if on each January 1, you could set inviolable rules about what you would and would not eat for the rest of the year. While this is a fairytale in the world of diet and exercise, it is absolutely within the power of investors.

I believe that as Barry Schwartz says, "…if 'constraint' sometimes affords a kind of liberation while 'freedom' affords a kind of enslavement, then people would be wise to seek out some measure of appropriate constraint."[111] Ego entreats us to concentrate our bets owing to our exceptional powers of thought and observation. Emotion tells us what we are feeling in the moment is the truest gauge of safety or danger. The talking heads on TV manufacture a new crisis daily, enticing us to focus on the lurid but unlikely, while our fear of loss and change whipsaws us between paralysis and overactivity. In an investment landscape so rife with behavioral risk, there is peace of mind to be found in consistency.

After all, as former Goldman Sachs model-maker Emanuel Derman says, "The similarity of physics and finance lies more in their syntax than their semantics. In physics you're playing against God, and He doesn't change His laws very often. In finance you're playing against God's creatures, agents who value assets based on their ephemeral opinions."[112]

What I am proposing here is that you consistently bet on inconsistency. What I am asking you to do is bet unfailingly on the failures of human reason, which is a sure bet indeed. It is a painful thing to admit that education, intellect and willpower are inadequate to make you the type of investor you would like to be, but it's not as painful as losing money.

What now?

Think—"Processes probably beat people."

Ask—"If I could automate some decisions (e.g., what to eat, what to wear), how might my outcomes in other areas be improved?"

Do—Set systematic parameters for buying, selling, holding and re-investing funds and follow them slavishly.

2. Clarity

"Simplicity is the ultimate sophistication."

—**Leonardo da Vinci**

Nassim Nicholas Taleb hilariously relates a story that speaks to how we think about innovation and how our best efforts to be creative can be thwarted by our tendency to overcomplicate. As Taleb points out, the wheel was created over 6000 years ago, but the wheeled suitcase was not invented until 1970. In fact, humankind even achieved manned space flight (May 5, 1961) before the invention of the wheeled suitcase!

For years, harried travelers would drag heavy bags through an airport unaided, doing untold damage to bodies and departure times. When relief initially came, it was in the form of a sort of wheeled exoskeleton to which bags could be lashed or bungee-corded; an improvement but still unnecessarily cumbersome. It is only in the last few decades that wheels have actually been placed on the luggage itself, a seemingly intuitive approach that only took us 6000 years to achieve.

Taleb says of this concept, "Both governments and universities have done very, very little for innovation and discovery, precisely because, in addition to their blinding rationalism, they look for the complicated, the lurid, the newsworthy, the narrated, the scientistic, and the grandiose, rarely for the wheel on the suitcase."[113] You've likely seen an invention or idea and thought, "Why didn't I think of that?!" The reason may have a great deal to do with trying too hard.

The road to Hell

There are a number of reasons—some nefarious, others not—why Wall Street tends to complicate the process of financial planning and investing. Wall Street's "fetish for complexity", as Dr. Brian Portnoy refers to it, is a mix of justifying fees, trying to make sense of a complicated system and falling prey to the mistaken notion that convolution equals sophistication. As H. L. Mencken quipped,

"What ails the truth is that it is mainly uncomfortable, and often dull. The human mind seeks something more amusing, and more caressing." Whatever the impetus, the road to poor returns is paved with complexity just as surely as the road to Hell is paved with good intentions. Motivations aside, complexity kills.

Barry Schwartz, author of *The Paradox of Choice*, studied what increasing complexity does to our ability to make good decisions and hit on three consistent themes.[114] Schwartz found that when confronted with complex decisions we spend more time and effort, make more mistakes and the consequences of our mistakes are more severe. Pair these findings with the reality that there are 45 times as many mutual fund options today as there were 50 years ago and you get a sense that most investors are facing an uphill climb when trying to determine how best to invest.[115]

It can be hard to embrace the call for simplicity in investment management in a world where complexity has brought us so much good. Fully one-third of my young son's peers will live to be over 100 years old and this lengthening of life has been brought about by complicated advancements in medicine and technology. IBM recently revealed that we are creating over 2.5 quintillion bytes of data each day. To put that into perspective, we now create more content every three days than we did in the two millennia from the year 0 to the year 2000! True, some of that content is cat videos, but this rich data also includes information that provides educational opportunities to the underserved and keeps governments and corporations accountable. Undoubtedly, the net effect of increasing complexity in technology and medicine has had a profound positive impact on the human family.

If complexity has been beneficial elsewhere, it seems plausible to suggest that this should also be the case for investors. After all, greater transparency and further knowledge are almost universally worthwhile elsewhere in life. Once again, Wall Street Bizarro World may prove the exception to the rule. Jason Zweig talks about how this glut of information has actually served to disconnect equity investing from what it truly is: partial ownership of a business. Zweig says:

"By pouring continuous data about stocks into bars and barbershops, kitchens and cafes, taxicabs and truck stops, financial websites and financial TV turned the stock market into a nonstop national video game. The public felt more knowledgeable about the markets than ever before. Unfortunately, while people were drowning in data, knowledge was nowhere to be found. Stocks became entirely decoupled from the companies that had issued them—pure abstractions, just blips moving across a TV or computer screen. If the blips were moving up, nothing else mattered."[116]

This overabundance of information, unleashed on an investing public not educated to critically examine it, has the effect of intensifying emotions more often than it truly enlightens the mind.

Every advance in technology brings with it a host of unintended consequences, some of which subvert the very reasons the technology exists in the first place. The advanced weaponry that protects our police and soldiers is also used to slaughter school children. The planes that allow us to visit relatives during the holidays also take us away from our families on frequent business travel. Similarly, the advances in financial technology that have given investors greater knowledge and compressed fees have also led to rampant short-termism and a DIY mentality that fails to account for our flawed psychology.

Consider chart 4, showing equity holding periods have just about halved every ten years for the past six decades. As trading has gotten easier and less expensive and financial news has become more plentiful, holding periods have dramatically shortened. This may not seem like a big deal until you realize that holding periods have a direct historical relationship with returns, with greater returns accruing to those who show more patience. As Nate Silver says of this concept, "We face danger whenever information growth outpaces our understanding of how to process it. The last 40 years of human history imply that it can still take a long time to translate information into useful knowledge, and that if we are not careful, we may take a step back in the meantime." Progress can and should be our friend, but we must ensure our technology does not outpace our psychology.

Chart 4—Stock holding periods by decade

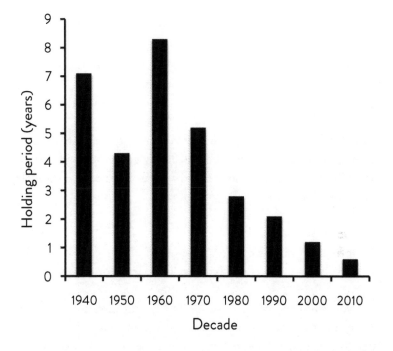

When less is more

Another consequence of financial information overload is that it leads to drawing spurious correlations between variables. As Nate Silver reports, the government produces data on 45,000 economic variables each year! Pair this reality with the fact that there are relatively few dramatic economic events (e.g., there have been 11 American recessions since the end of World War II) and you get what Silver refers to as putting data into a blender and calling the result haute cuisine.[117]

In a world of big data, we all too often fail to see the forest of "is this a good business?" for looking at the trees of esoteric data points. No matter what exotic economic measures professors and pundits may dream up in the future, there will always be some that show a fleeting correlation with stock returns but fail to pass the sniff test of "Should it matter when determining whether or not to become partial owner of a business?"

Daniel Kahneman and Amos Tversky's "Linda the Bank Teller" study provides a powerful example of how more information is not always better. The two researchers set out to prove something that they had observed empirically—emotional signals can overwhelm probability. We now refer to this as "base rate fallacy". The two men posed the question:

Linda is 31-years-old, single, outspoken and very bright. She majored in philosophy. As a student, she was deeply concerned with issues of discrimination and social justice, and also participated in anti-nuclear demonstrations.

Which is more probable?
1. Linda is a bank teller.
2. Linda is a bank teller and is active in the feminist movement.

If you consider the question rationally and probabilistically, you understand that the number of feminist bank tellers is a subset of the larger population of bank tellers. But most people answered that (2) is more likely, falling victim to a host of noise among the true signal of probability. Our minds are populated with preconceptions about the type of people that are involved in the feminist movement and Linda checks many of those boxes.

Just as more information about Linda made us less capable of judging what really mattered, so much of what passes as investment advice is marketing or clickbait with a thin educational veneer. A part of any sensible approach to security selection is determining what matters most and a focus on those variables to the exclusion of the cacophony all around. If everything matters, nothing does.

Andrew Haldane, Executive Director of Monetary Analysis and Statistics at the Bank of England, makes a compelling academic argument for simplicity in his speech, 'The Dog and the Frisbee'. Haldane begins his comments by relating the example of catching a Frisbee, a process that "requires the catcher to weigh a complex array of physical and atmospheric factors, among them wind speed and Frisbee rotation." His question: how is such a complicated process attainable by most humans and even more admirably performed by dogs? The answer lies in the use of a simple rule of thumb—run at a speed that keeps the moving disc roughly at eye level. Haldane argues that the more complex a problem, the more simple the solution must be to avoid what statisticians call "overfitting."

Haldane gives a number of examples of overfitting, beginning with complicated sports betting algorithms that examine historical measures of performance. He finds that such complex approaches are beaten by a recognition heuristic—simply picking the name of the player or the team that you have heard of. He goes on to relate that, "experimental evidence has found the same to be true across a range of other activities. Among physicians diagnosing heart attacks, simple decision trees beat a complex model. Among detectives locating serial criminals, simple locational rules trump complex psychological profiling... and among shopkeepers understanding repeat purchase data out-predict complex models." Complex problems yield noisy results that can only be understood using big-picture, simplifying frameworks.

Haldane contrasts rules for governing known risks versus operating in a situation fraught with uncertainty, like investing in the stock market. He says, "Under risk, policy should respond to every raindrop; it is fine-tuned. Under uncertainty, that logic is reversed. Complex environments often instead call for simple decision rules. That is because these rules are more robust to ignorance. Under uncertainty, policy may only respond to every thunderstorm; it is coarse-tuned." It is precisely because the variables impacting the market are so varied and complex that it requires a simple set of rules for mastery. Just as a human trying to calculate velocity, rotation, wind speed and trajectory would drop the Frisbee, an investor mired in every piece of market minutiae is doomed to both a prodigious headache and poor performance.

Does big data = big money?

Another danger in complexity is that it is commonly conflated with the potential for big returns. The tendency to do so is a result of the mistaken notion that complex systems like the stock market require equally complex solutions. However, quite the opposite is true. As Albert Einstein says, "We can not solve our problems with the same level of thinking that created them."

It is true that the market is a complex dynamic system with inputs so myriad they are impossible to account for. It is further true that the dynamism of markets and their participants is such that you "never cross the same stream twice." Attempting to attend to market minutiae is a recipe for insanity, frustration and wasted time (to say nothing of the fees).

Unnecessary complexity also brings about unseen complications, as was evidenced in the 2007–09 financial crisis. Financial products were packaged and repackaged into what Warren Buffett referred to as "financial weapons of mass destruction." In many cases, those selling and even creating the products had very little idea what they had assembled, much less how it might interact with the larger financial system. Nassim Taleb, who has written persuasively on the "fragilizing" effects of unneeded complexity says, "A complex system, contrary to what people believe, does not require complicated systems and regulations and intricate policies. The simpler, the better. Complications lead to multiplicative chains of unanticipated effects... Yet simplicity has been difficult to implement in modern life because it is against the spirit of a certain brand of people who seek sophistication so they can justify their profession."

Complexity does many things—it gives Wall Street an excuse to charge you more and it justifies the professions of people adding marginal to negative value—it just turns out that none of those things are good for end investors. As Ben Carlson says, "Simplicity trumps complexity. Conventional gives you much better odds than exotic. A long-term process is more important than short-term outcomes. And perspective goes much further than tactics."[118] The great paradox of investing is that the only rational response to the enormous complexity of the markets is to do a few of the most important things very well and with absolute consistency.

Complicating investment management appeals to the human longing for sophistication but does little to help and much to hurt investors.

What now?

Think—"Some is better than none, but a little is better than a lot."
Ask—"What are the three to seven important facets of this decision?"
Do—Ignore all noise that falls outside of the three to seven facets mentioned above.

---

60 seconds

Take a moment and think about the person or people in your life that mean the most to you—your partner, your children, your parents. In less than one minute describe out loud what it is they mean to you and why they mean so much. Not hard to do is it?

Now, take that same 60 seconds and explain to me how you would go about evaluating the desirability of an investment. Many of you may be able to do this with ease, but most of us find this a far more complicated exercise than talking about something deeply meaningful like a cherished relationship. There is no better barometer of real interest or mastery than an ability to simply explain a concept. Whether we are talking about love, baseball or the movement of the planets, the truly interested and deeply fluent are capable of simplifying the abstract.

That being so, call up your financial advisor out of the blue and ask him or her for their 60-second take on how they manage your money. If they can't give you a coherent answer in a minute or less, odds are that they either lack fluency or a systematic approach (which is bad news either way). Worse yet, if they give you a mouthful of overly complicated nonsense or suggest that it's beyond your comprehension, it may really be time to look for someone new. As Ben Carlson says, "The longer it takes someone to explain their investing approach, the worse off it tends to be, but the more intelligent it sounds to unsuspecting investment consumers."

Now, before we move on, you really ought to call that important person in your life and tell them why they are so great.

3. Courageousness

"Courage is being scared to death… and saddling up anyway."

—John Wayne

Jason Zweig's humorous book *The Devil's Financial Dictionary* satirizes Wall Street culture and the accompanying jargon. Some of Zweig's wittier definitions include **DAY TRADER**, *n.* See **IDIOT**, and **MUTUAL FUND**, *n.* A fund that is not equal: its investors share all risks equally, whereas its managers share all fees exclusively.

Although Zweig did not include **COURAGE** in his financial dictionary, I'd like to think his definition might look something like, "The most talked about and least present of all virtues on Wall Street." My young daughter knows that stocks should be bought low and sold high, yet the evidence across retail and institutional contexts is clear that investors do just the opposite and tend to time the market horribly. Therefore, a system aimed at correcting our most basic human impulses must guide us toward courage in two very specific ways: it must lead us to take non-consensus views and should keep us invested almost all of the time.

It pays to be different

The reason for the first of the two conditions just mentioned is simple: better results take different thinking. Value investing pioneer Ben Graham quipped, "the investor who selects issues chiefly on the basis of this year's superior results, or on what he is told he may expect for next year, is likely to find that others have done the same thing for the same reasons. To enjoy a reasonable chance for continued better than average results, the investor must follow policies which are 1. Inherently sound and promising 2. Not popular on Wall Street."[119] Howard Marks echoes Graham: "to achieve superior investment results, you have to hold nonconsensus views regarding value, and they have to be accurate."[120] The only way to beat the crowd is to be different than the crowd, which is easier said than done for a species that gains much (outside of investing) from togetherness and mimicry. It has been rightly said that good investors spend a lot of their time being ridiculed and lonely. As Seth Klarman noted, "You don't become a value investor for the group hugs."[121]

One measure of courage is "active share," introduced by Cremers and Petajisto in their seminal paper, 'How Active is Your Fund Manager? A New Measure That Predicts Performance'.[122] Active share is an intuitive but powerful measure, "which represents the share of portfolio holdings that differ from the benchmark index holdings." Basically, how courageous is the manager being with respect to holding non-consensus views and exposing herself to tracking error? Examining 2650 funds over a 23-year period, the two Yale professors found the most courageous funds (i.e., those with 80% or greater active share) outperformed by between 2% and 2.7% per year—courage paid off!

As I have repeated throughout the book, knowing the right thing to do has very little to do with actually doing it, which is why courage is aided by other principles discussed here like consistency and conviction. By automating the process of security selection—consistency—we lessen our ability to chicken out and make crowded trades. By holding a concentrated portfolio—conviction—we decrease the likelihood that we will simply end up with a portfolio that mirrors the benchmark.

Doing something by doing nothing

Courage is not limited to simply having contrarian views. It also means hanging on for the volatile ride over the long term when getting off of the psychic rollercoaster would be so much easier.

The appeal of jumping in and out of the market at just the right times is undeniable. After all, as Quartz says in its article on perfect market timing in 2013, "A trader who began the year with $1,000 in her brokerage account and put all of her money in each day's best-performing equity in the S&P 500—day after day—for the 241 trading days so far this year would have $264 billion in her account today."[123] We all understand that level of precision is unworkable, but even taking the more macro approach of precisely timing huge dips and vertical leaps is awfully appealing on paper (not to mention that it looks really easy with 20/20 hindsight), but awfully hard to perfect in practice.

Unsystematic market timing is a fool's errand and we have the research to prove it. A study of over 200 market-timing newsletters found that their timing calls were right just south of one-quarter of the time.[124] A similar study by two Duke professors found that by following only the best 10% of all market-timing newsletters, you could have earned a 12.6% annualized return from 1991 to 1995. However, someone who had ignored market timers altogether and simply bought the index would have gotten 16.4% annualized over that same time period. Even the best market-timers underperformed the "lazy investor"! Professor H. Negat Seybun found that 95% of large market gains over a 30-year timeframe came from a paltry 90 of the 7500 trading days studied. If you had been out of the market on what amounted to just over 1% of the total trading days—perhaps by getting your attempts at market timing slightly wrong—you would have experienced negligible returns over that period.[125]

Even following some fairly sensible rules has been proven ineffective, as evidenced by excellent reporting by the blog 538.[126] It says of returns from 1980 to 2015, "Imagine two people who each invested $1,000 in the S&P 500 at the beginning of 1980. The first one buys once and never sells. The second one is slightly more cautious: He sells any time the market loses 5% in a week, and buys back in once it rebounds 3% from wherever it bottoms out. At the end of last week, the first investor's holdings would be worth $18,635. The second investor would have just $10,613." The problem is that although the market has crashed with some regularity—almost 100 declines of 3% or more in a single day and 24 in which it fell over 5% in a single day—it has bounced back with equal regularity. As the blog says, "...every one of those declines has been followed by a rebound. Sometimes it comes right away. Sometimes it takes weeks or months. But when it comes, it comes quickly. If you wait until the rebound is clearly visible, you've already missed the biggest gains."

An old investing saw says time in the market is more important than timing the market and in this case the folk wisdom seems to be right on. Burton Malkiel shares that the market has risen over three times as much as it has fallen, meaning that "the odds of being successful when you are in cash rather than stocks are almost three to one against you."[127] Rock star mutual fund manager Peter Lynch conducted a study that looked at the 30-year period from 1965 to 1995 and found that timing had very little impact for long-term investors. Lynch found that if you invested every year at the lowest day of the market, your return over that time would have been 11.7% annualized versus 11% annualized for those who had invested on the most expensive day of the year. Not too dramatic a result, especially when considering the unlikelihood of a real investor being able to systematically invest at the worst possible time (the most expensive day for the market) every year.

But for all of the evidence that tactical investing is difficult, the student of market psychology finds himself at an awkward crossroads. He understands market timing is ineffectual but is also aware of times in history when broad market levels have become obviously and grossly disconnected from any measure of fundamental value. From the Roaring 20s and the Nifty Fifty to the Tech Bubble and the Housing Crisis, periods of mania have been relatively frequent, easy to spot with typical valuation metrics and have had dramatic wealth-destroying effects.

Therefore, if the rule is "don't time the market," is it possible that there are ever exceptions to the rule? I believe that there are and that consistent with our emphasis on courageousness, they are infrequent, painful to implement and will run directly contrary to what feels right. The perversity of risk is that it is most present when it is least felt.

Avoiding catastrophic loss

Over the past 100 years, the ability of the global economy to create and compound wealth has staggered the mind and stymied the permanently pessimistic. But the blossoming of global prosperity has not occurred without significant stretches of scorched-Earth volatility. Indeed, as Meb Faber points out, "all of the G-7 countries have experienced at least one period where stocks lost 75% of their value. The unfortunate mathematics of a 75% decline require an investor to realize a 300% gain just to get back to even."[128] He goes on to say:

"Individuals invested in U.S. stocks in the late 1920s and early 1930s, German asset classes in the 1910s and 1940s, Russian stocks in 1927, Chinese stocks in 1949, U.S. real estate in the mid-1950s, Japanese stocks in the 1980s, emerging markets and commodities in the late 1990s, and nearly everything in 2008, would reason that holding these assets was a decidedly unwise course of action. Most individuals do not have a sufficiently long time frame to recover from large drawdowns from risky asset classes."

Buy and hold makes sense for most people most of the time, but this is no guarantee that your timeline or context will make it sound advice for you in particular. As chart 5 shows, the stock market has, with some consistency, gone 15 years at a time with little to negative real growth. If you were to buy and hold during these periods, it wouldn't look like such a good strategy.

Many investors, steeped in the buy and hold tradition, will find it irksome that I am suggesting there are instances, however rare, when investors should seek safety and get more conservative. Many will point to the example of Warren Buffett who has said repeatedly that his favorite holding period is "forever" as someone assiduously averse to any form of market timing.

Chart 5—S&P 500 real (inflation adjusted) growth of $1

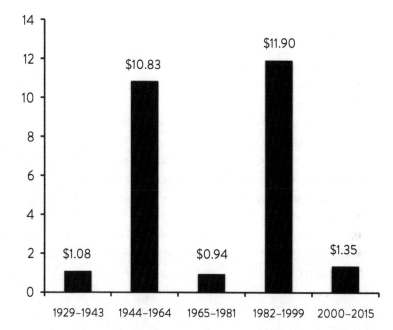

However, Buffett's words are a classic case of "do as I say not as I do." In late 2019, Berkshire was sitting on a huge pile of cash (over $120 billion).[129] The Oracle is not an "all stocks all the time" investor, but rather a thoughtful allocator who, let's face it, times the market. As David Rolfe says of The Oracle, "The guy's just not going to spend the cash to spend it. (He's) the best market timer I ever saw."[130]

A less pithy but more pertinent quote can be found in Buffett's 1992 Berkshire Hathaway Chairman's Letter: "The investment shown by the discounted-flows-of-cash calculation to be the cheapest is the one that the investor should purchase... Moreover, though the value equation has usually shown equities to be cheaper than bonds, that result is not inevitable: When bonds are calculated to be the more attractive investment, they should be bought."

It's all well and good to suggest that we should be on guard against bubbles that presage catastrophic wealth destruction and use an element of market timing to avoid them, but what exactly are we looking for? There are six variables I examine when looking for asset bubbles, with the caveat that it is extremely rare for them to occur in concert (which is why it is extremely rare that investors should seek to get defensive):

1. **Exceedingly steep valuations**—the price of stocks has been meaningfully above their average preceding every major crash in US history.
2. **Excessive leverage**—both consumers and businesses take on unusually large debt loads during periods of easy money.
3. **Lax lending standards**—frothy markets lessen the perception of risk and lending standards tend to relax accordingly.
4. **Nearly universal bullish sentiment**—positive psychology is both a cause and effect of prosperity and it becomes self-perpetuating.
5. **Low volatility**—indicates complacency on the part of investors who have become accustomed to high returns with little effort.
6. **High participation in risk assets**—soaring prices naturally increase the percentage of equity holdings, but investors also tend to be overweight stocks at exactly the wrong times.

If these six variables are early indications of a bubble, their deterioration is likewise a sign that the bubble is starting to burst. As sentiment, momentum and valuations begin to crumble from previously astronomical levels, it may be wise to consider a more defensive posture.

Sinning a little

Peter Lynch correctly quipped that, "far more money has been lost by investors preparing for corrections or trying to anticipate corrections, than has been lost in corrections themselves."[131] But as Jesse Felder points out in his *Felder Report*, it should be noted that Lynch's milieu must be taken into account when assessing his record and advice. Lynch's career, spanning from 1977 to 1990, included a period during which equities hovered right at one standard deviation below their average valuation (as measured by market cap to GDP). By comparison, we currently find ourselves more than two standard deviations *above* the average by that very same measure.

In fact, the most richly valued month in Lynch's career (September 1987) is directly comparable to the absolute nadir of the last 15 years (March 2009). Periods of cheap valuation like the markets Lynch lived through lead to positive forward returns and make buy and hold approaches very attractive. Just as a six foot tall man can drown in a river that is three feet deep on average, investors can drown in equity markets that average 10% a year returns over long periods of time.

The rule-based behavioral approach seeks first and foremost to tilt probability in favor of the investor, which means that the default behavior for market participants should be patience, calm and inactivity. Likewise, any rules aimed at reducing market participation should lead to infrequent action and look for every excuse to stay invested.

The Philosophical Economics blog suggests an interesting twist on market timing—specifically, looking at market timing in much the same way that we consider asset allocation.[132] An investor with a long-term 40/60 allocation to stocks and cash would have little hope of an impressive return, tilted as they are toward safety. Likewise, any system that keeps investors on the sidelines 60% of the time will harm their performance dramatically. However, just as a prudent investor might keep a small portion of her wealth in low-risk assets for protection of principal and sanity, a behavioral investor can follow a systematic process for infrequently taking risk off of the table when the market is poised to do its worst.

Indiscriminate, gut-level, frequent activity is a sin, no doubt, but as the late economist Paul Samuelson is rumored to have said in the late 1990s, "Market timing is an investment sin, and for once I recommend that you sin a little."[133]

What now?

Think—"The best thing to do is often, but not always, nothing."
Ask—"Is my fear (greed) aligned with or contrary to that of the crowd?"
Do—Become gradually more defensive as stocks become two to three standard deviations disconnected from their long-term valuations.

4. Conviction

"Wide diversification is only required when investors do not understand what they are doing."

—**Warren Buffett**

The fourth and final characteristic of an RBI portfolio is that it ought to be convicted. While the mention of the word convict in financial circles can conjure images of Bernie Madoff, what I'm referring to here is that your portfolio ought to have conviction. Specifically, it should exist somewhere between the hubris of owning one or two stocks and the passivity of owning every stock. Dr. Tom Howard explains:

"At one extreme is the decision to purchase all stocks in the market and weight them according to their market capitalization. This is known as an index portfolio and its performance is determined exclusively by the overall performance of the stock market and not by individual stock performance. The other extreme is to invest everything in one stock and thus bet on the singular performance of this one company. You are seeking the right balance between these two extremes."[134]

Owning one stock is what you ought to do if truths about equities were perfectly knowable. Why diversify if you could objectively pick the best of the best? By contrast, owning every stock (i.e., an index fund) is what you ought to do if truths about stocks were entirely unknowable.

If doing fundamental research, looking at prices, exploring business practices and the like gives you no edge in determining that one stock is better than the other, buy them all and bet on the larger growth of the economy.

The best practice lies somewhere in the middle. There are judgments we can make about the quality of an investment, but these judgments must be tempered by an acknowledgement of their imperfection as well as the tendency of market participants to act irrationally. Thus, a convicted basket of between 25 and 50 stocks offers the simultaneous potential for outperformance as well as real differentiation from the index.

Goldilocks diversification

Note that diversification should always occur within and between asset classes. What we are discussing here relates to the domestic equity piece of your overall investing pie. You should not concentrate your overall wealth in a portfolio of 25 stocks; it should be spread between foreign stocks, domestic stocks, real estate investment trusts and the like. However, as few as 25 stocks could comprise your diversified allocation to domestic equities.

For those unfamiliar with the idea that relatively few stocks can provide a great deal of diversification, the thought of owning a high-conviction portfolio can seem terrifying. But just as surely as pollsters can get a representative sample of tens of millions of voters by talking to a few hundred, you can own a diversified piece of the US equity market with just a few dozen stocks.

One of the earliest studies to speak to this reality was conducted by John Evans and Stephen Archer of the University of Washington. Evans and Archer found that the benefits of diversification dropped off precipitously when more than 20 stocks were added to a portfolio.[135] Further, billionaire investor Joel Greenblatt says in his book *You Can Be a Stock Market Genius* that nonmarket (i.e., diversifiable) risk is reduced by 46% by owning just two stocks, 72% with four stocks, 81% with eight stocks and 93% with as few as 16 stocks.[136] Greenblatt's work shows just how quickly most of the benefits of diversification can be achieved and also how quickly they begin to erode after about the 20 stock point. Ben Graham says it nicely: "There should be adequate though not excessive diversification. This might mean a minimum of ten different issues and a maximum of about thirty."[137]

Figure 4 illustrates these ideas about diversification. Rule-based behavioral investing advocates a just right—or Goldilocks—diversification position between overconfidence and the mistaken idea that the price is always right.

Figure 4—Just right diversification around the level of 25 stocks

ONE STOCK	25 STOCKS	ALL STOCKS
Potential outperformance, dramatic business risk	Potential outperformance, minimal business risk	No potential for outperformance, minimal business risk

Active in passive clothing

An investor who fails to appropriately diversify is a speculator whose ego is not in check. An investor who excessively diversifies is giving up valuable return potential for a very small degree of risk reduction. A behavioral investor wants the best of both risk reduction and return and seeks that in the form of a portfolio that is diversified with conviction.

I have said before and will say again that passive investing is a sensible route to take for the investor most concerned with adequate performance at a reasonable price. But for those who seek outsized performance, high conviction is the only way to go for the simple reason that, as Sir John Templeton says, "It is impossible to produce a superior performance unless you do something different than the majority."

Unfortunately, much of what passes for active management today is not active at all. Closet indexing, as passive-in-active-clothing is called, leaves investors with the worst of all possible worlds—high fees without meaningful differentiation—and the problem is more widespread than most imagine. Tom Howard of AthenaInvest found in his exploration of closet indexing that, "For the typical fund, low-conviction positions outnumber high-conviction positions by three-to-one."[138] Dr. Wesley Gray of Alpha Architect found that just 8% of ETFs and 23% of mutual funds differed meaningfully from their benchmarks. What's more, Gray found that the more active a fund was, the more expensive it tended to be, with fees for truly actively managed funds clocking in at an average of 128 basis points.[139] The research is clear that the vast majority of actively managed funds do not differ meaningfully from their benchmarks and those that do make investors pay handsomely for this.

If the ostensible mandate of an active manager is to outperform his benchmark, how is it that so many of their funds end up looking just like expensive versions of the index itself? The answer lies primarily in a silly concept known as tracking error. Tracking error is the degree to which a portfolio deviates from the benchmark against which it is compared and, for reasons unclear to me, is seen as a form of investment risk. That's right, the active fund manager is simultaneously expected to beat the benchmark without being that much different than it.

As James Montier says of this foolishness, "The use of such measures as tracking error for an active manager is akin to sending a boxer into the ring with instructions to make sure he is always within a point or two of his opponent, rather than with the aim of trying to win the bout."[140] Although tracking error is framed as risk more broadly, the true risk is to the career of the fund manager. Christopher H. Browne explained it well in his 2000 address to Columbia Business School:

> "Investment performance is generally measured against a benchmark, and claims to being long-term investors aside, the typical institutional client tracks performance on a monthly or quarterly basis versus the benchmark. Performance that deviates from the benchmark becomes suspect and can lead to termination of the money manager. Consistency of returns

relative to the benchmark are more important than absolute performance especially in a world dominated by the hypothesis that asset allocation is more important than stock selection. Once the advisor figures out how he or she is being measured, they realize that tailoring the portfolio to the benchmark reduces the risk of relative underperformance and loss of the account. Unfortunately, the chances of significantly outperforming the benchmark are equally diminished."[141]

Investors seeking benchmark-like returns can have their wish granted for as little as 3 basis points by the large fund families. However, for those of us seeking returns in excess of the benchmark, we must exorcise the notion of tracking error as a form of risk. As I wrote in *Personal Benchmark*, "As long as the benchmark remains the gold standard, savvy money managers will be reticent to take non-normative bets and go against the grain, no matter how big an opportunity they may sense."[142] John Maynard Keynes noted that it is "better for reputation to fail conventionally than to succeed unconventionally", a reality that has been embraced by fund managers presented with an impossibly conflicted mandate. The rule-based behavioral investor understands that high conviction, differentiated investing is the only kind worth paying for and that index returns ought to be bought at index prices.

Active management works

The evidence suggests that high-conviction is the way to deliver outperformance. Meredith Jones is an internationally-recognized researcher in the alternative investment industry and the author of *Women of the Street*, an in-depth analysis of the factors shared by the best female asset managers. In her examination of the best of the best, Jones observed the following: "The women interviewed for this book tend to run what is known in investing as 'high conviction' portfolios. This means that a portfolio may be diversified into a number of positions, but it will not choose so many investments that the portfolio returns become diluted by picking second, third and fourth-tier ideas."[143]

Although specifically relating to female fundies, Jones' observations bear out across the board. Cohen, Polk and Silli found that a fund's best idea (as determined by position size) generated averaged annualized outperformance of 6% per year. Even more importantly, they found that performance decreased in a stepwise fashion as position size decreased![144] Much of the conversation around active managers' historical underperformance has drawn the erroneous conclusion that these managers do not have stock picking skill. To the contrary, it would seem that much of what besets active managers is not the ability to successfully pick stocks, but the courage to pick them in concentrated enough doses that they lead to successful outperformance.

The need to diversify within and between asset classes is a hallmark of behavioral investing, but it need not doom investors to mediocre returns. By introducing a bit of science and nuance into the conversation, we begin to realize that diversification and conviction can coexist. As Warren Buffett has said, "The goal of each investor, should be to create a portfolio that will deliver him or her the highest possible look-through earnings a decade or so from now." Too much diversification is a drag on performance and too little risks far too much. If diversification is the "eat your vegetables" of investing, high conviction diversification adds a little spice.

What now?

Think—"Diverse enough to be humble, convicted enough to count."
Ask –"Am I paying active fees for passive management?"
Do—Diversify within your 25–30 stock portfolio by ensuring that no single sector is overrepresented.

The funnel

The creation of an RBI approach can be conceptualized as a funnel consisting of three steps that work toward greater and greater specificity. Our first step in designing a program of behavioral asset management was to enumerate and codify the universe of behavioral risk. Having done so, we set out to create a process by which we could minimize the presence of the five facets of behavioral risk. This process can be easily remembered as four Cs: Consistency, Clarity, Courageousness and Conviction.

Consistency ensures that we systematically avoid all five facets of behavioral risk rather than leaving this up to our education or willpower. Clarity addresses information risk and attention risk by focusing our efforts on the simple-but-probable variables rather than the salient-but-unlikely pieces of data that tend to find favor in discretionary approaches. Emotion and conservation risks lead us to time the market poorly by following our fears and feelings rather than the RBI approach of data-informed Courageousness. Finally, if we are to outperform (which is the only reason to be an active investor), we must follow a policy of high-Conviction investing that avoids the hubris of too little diversification (ego risk) and the irrational, fear-based need to own the entire market (emotion risk).

We now understand the behavioral risks to guard against and the process by which to construct a portfolio, which leads us to a very important question—what methods should be used to determine the constituents of this portfolio?

The Five Ps
of Investing

"All models are wrong, but some models are useful."

—George E. P. Box

ARMED WITH THE knowledge of your behavioral weaknesses and a process for overcoming them, all you lack now is the small matter of knowing what you are looking for when selecting a group of individual securities. What follows is my best attempt, rooted in the bedrock of research, to insert "what works on Wall Street" into a rule-based behavioral framework. This is where we turn to the five Ps of equity investing.

While I believe that the five factors presented here are powerful and enduring, I am not suggesting this is the only right way to approach equity selection. There are many successful ways to select securities and it is far more important that you follow a consistent, convicted, courageous, clear approach than that you include a specific set of factors. Following a sensible recipe is more important than the specific ingredients you choose.

In laying the groundwork for the five most essential considerations in creating an RBI portfolio, you must be aware of two important truths:

1. The aim of the five Ps is to tilt probability in your favor when selecting stocks.
2. It won't always work.

I have referenced a gambling analogy before and will do so again here, because becoming a successful behavioral investor looks a great deal like being The House instead of The Drunken Vacationer. Contrary to popular belief, The House does not win every time or even anything like every time. Depending on the game in question, The House may only come out ahead slightly more than 50% of the time. However, they know that a disciplined process, repeated frequently and consistently, can yield powerful results. Think of the power of slightly-better-than-average odds the next time you marvel at the gaudy grandeur of one of Vegas's temples of irrationality.

Likewise, rule-based investing is about making simple, systematic tweaks to your investment portfolio to try and get an extra percentage point or two that has a dramatic positive impact on managing risk and compounding your wealth over time. As Nate Silver says: "Successful gamblers—and successful forecasters of any kind—do not think of the future in terms of no-lose bets, unimpeachable theories, and infinitely precise measurements. These are the illusions of the sucker, the sirens of his overconfidence. Successful gamblers, instead, think of the future as speckles of probability, flickering upward and downward like a stock market ticker to every new jolt of information."[145]

Let me say with all forthrightness that the RBI model is not perfect and that some years following its principles won't even beat a passive market cap weighted index. But what it does do is tilt the odds in your favor by consistently exploiting the psychological failings of your opponents in the market. Over time, hundreds of anomalies— or return distortions based on some quirk or another—have been discovered in financial markets. What separates the very few persistent anomalies that endure from their evanescent kin is that human behavior keeps them around. The five Ps take advantage of these persistent behavioral anomalies by being timeless, commonsensical and, most importantly, rooted in well-worn psychological tendencies that ensure their longevity.

The very fact that RBI offers a sensible middle ground will make it unattractive to many investors. Passive evangelists and efficient market advocates will feel that any attempt to out-think the market will end badly, leading them to opt out. On the other extreme, some will insist that they will consistently be able to pick the handful of greatest stocks year in and year out (despite all of the evidence to the contrary), meaning that they will eschew something as boring as simply "tilting the odds in your favor."

For our part, we will settle for the unsexy if profitable approach of trying to do a few important things very well. Statistician Nate Silver agrees (at least with respect to cards): "getting a few basic things right can go a long way. In poker, for instance, simply learning to fold your worst hands, bet your best ones, and make some effort to consider what your opponent holds will substantially mitigate your losses. If you are willing to do this, then perhaps 80% of the time you will be making the same decision as one of the best poker players... even if you have spent only 20% as much time studying the game." By consistently buying stocks that exhibit characteristics of historical outperformance with roots in human behavior, you can have both very nice returns and a very nice life that is altogether free of the tedium of becoming a stock analyst.

Before introducing the model in earnest, I want to anticipate one objection to the RBI approach from the outset: some will think that it is too easy. The fact that we are looking at five simple variables in an ocean of big data will strike some as simple-minded and the fact that the guy suggesting it is from Alabama will only further their incredulity. But I am not alone in my call for the power of a few simple rules and variables. Financial advisor Martin Whitman opines, "Based on my own personal experience—both as an investor in recent years and an expert witness in years past—rarely do more than three or four variables really count. Everything else is noise."[146]

Similarly, Warren Buffett has put together one of the most extraordinary track records in the world by following a few simple rules that he learned in graduate school. As he says, "Having sound principles takes you through everything. And the bedrock principles that really I learned from Graham and Dodd, I haven't had to do anything with them. They take me through good periods, they take me through bad periods. In the end, I don't worry about them because I know they work."[147]

Lastly, you might like to think in terms of a great chef and a great investor having a lot in common. They master a handful of broadly applicable techniques and administer them to perfection.

Enough preamble, let's look at the five Ps of stock selection in greater detail.

Are you stupid?

"You're stupid."

"You are wrong."

"I know better than you."

Being a zero sum game, this is what people are saying to you every time that you buy or sell a stock. Scarier still, over 70% of the people impugning your intelligence over a buy or sell decision are professional investors that have you beat with respect to technology and information (in addition to the less-relevant edge they enjoy with respect to pomade and pinstriped suits).

Your only hope against such a formidable opponent is an edge based in psychology. You can't compete on speed, access or market education, so you are left to compete on discipline and mental toughness. Warren Buffett's favorite teacher said of such discipline, "What's needed is first a definite rule for purchasing which indicates a priori that you're acquiring stocks for less than they're worth. Second, you have to operate with a large enough number of stocks to make the approach effective. And finally you need a very definite guideline for selling."[148]

The RBI model meets each of Ben Graham's criteria; all you need to supply is the discipline. As I discuss each of the five pillars I will touch on both empirical and philosophical evidence of their efficacy. After all, we want enduring factors that are rooted in common sense, not some random alignment of variables. Well-educated, hyper-competitive stock jocks are calling you foolish every time they sell you a share—this is how you prove them wrong.

The five Ps of stock selection are:

1. Price
2. Properties
3. Pitfalls
4. People
5. Push

1. Never overpay (PRICE)

On a blustery winter day in Salt Lake City, I learned perhaps the most important lesson of my career—price impacts perceived quality. I had just finished giving a seminar at The Grand America to a group of financial advisors interested in applying behavioral finance to their practices. I was pleased with my overall performance, gratified by the response of the participants and was enjoying a celebratory Diet Coke outside of the conference room when I was approached by the man who had hired me to speak.

Expecting warm congratulations on a job well done, I instead was greeted with an abrupt, "People think you suck."

"Excuse me?" I said, sure that I'd done a little better than that in what I'd read to be a very successful session. He went on, "I want to be able to use you more in the field, but people in the home office assume you suck because your fees are too low. Having never met you, they see what you charge and assume you must be awful. People think you suck."

We walked to a lounge in the hotel where he went on to encourage me to triple or quadruple my asking price without changing one thing about my presentation. His thought was that if I evidenced a belief in my own abilities by charging more, others would be similarly persuaded. With a great deal of fear, I tripled my speaking fees following that meeting and have since more than quintupled my salary. While I hope that my presentation style has changed and improved somewhat over the years, I am essentially the same schmuck today that I was when I was charging far less. But by understanding an important truth about humans—that price determines perceived value—I have been able to create a nice career. Hopefully, fewer people think I suck too.

My anecdotal experience of price driving perception was proven much more artfully by the work of a "horizontal wine tasting" conducted by Stanford Professor Baba Shiv.[149] Shiv had participants lie on their backs in an fMRI machine and gave them carefully titrated doses of wine, each with an accompanying price tag. He then measured the brain activity of the participants as they sipped each of the wines, looking for a relationship between price and cerebral processing. Specifically, Shiv wanted to examine the part of the brain, the ventral medial prefrontal cortex, that we know codes for pleasure.

Sure enough, participants showed more activity in the pleasure centers of the brain when they thought they were drinking $90 wine versus $10 wine. The only problem was that it was all $10 wine! The participants were given the same wine in each condition, meaning the differences in pleasurable brain activity were attributable directly to perceived differences in price rather than the quality of the wine itself. All else being equal, we look to price as the foremost determinant of quality.

This tendency to conflate price with quality may lead us to overpay for clothing, cars or coffee, but is overall fairly harmless in terms of our retail purchases. In investing, it is disastrous. The polling organization Gallup periodically surveys American investors to determine whether or not they think now is a good time to invest. Gallup has found a strong correlation between the responses to this survey and the returns of the stock market, but it's just the opposite of what you'd hope for.

When Americans think that now is a good time to buy, stocks tend to be toward their peak expensiveness, meaning that medium-term results tend to be poor. As Nate Silver writes, "The highest figure that Gallup ever recorded in their survey was in January 2000, when a record high of 67% of Americans thought it was a good time to invest. Just two months later, the NASDAQ and other stock indices began to crash. Conversely, only 26% of Americans thought it was a good time to buy stocks in February 1990—but the S&P 500 almost quadrupled in value over the next ten years."[150]

Just as with wine and public speakers, the richer the valuations of the stock market, the better we think it will be. Unlike wine and speakers, there is actually an inverse relationship between price and performance in stocks—the more you pay, the less you get, period.

While it may negatively impact our perception of quality, it is a near universal truth that when things are on sale elsewhere, we tend to buy more of them. If your closet is anything like mine, it is littered with clothes that you bought because they were cheap, not necessarily because you loved or needed them. The stock market seems to be the demonstrable exception to this rule, a truth that is much to the detriment of investors.

Warren Buffett illustrates this point nicely in his typically folksy way with the example of hamburgers. He asks, "If you plan to eat hamburgers throughout your life and are not a cattle producer, should you wish for higher or lower prices for beef?" The answer is clear: consumers of hamburgers should hope for the lowest prices possible. He goes on:

"But now for the final exam: If you expect to be a net saver during the next five years, should you hope for a higher or lower stock market during that period? Many investors get this one wrong. Even though they are going to be net buyers of stocks for many years to come, they are elated when stock prices rise and depressed when they fall. In effect, they rejoice because prices have risen for 'hamburgers' they will soon be buying. This reaction makes no sense. Only those who will be sellers of equities in the near future should be happy at seeing stocks rise. Prospective purchasers should much prefer sinking prices."[151]

A value investor like Buffett, Howard Marks couches the danger of overpaying thusly: "Investing is a popularity contest, and the most dangerous thing is to buy something at the peak of its popularity. At that point, all favorable facts and opinions are already factored into its price, and no new buyers are left to emerge. The safest and most potentially profitable thing is to buy something when no one likes it. Given time, its popularity, and thus its price, can only go one way: up."[152] I cannot say this emphatically enough—paying an appropriate price, commonly referred to as value investing, is the single greatest thing that you can do to ensure appropriate returns and manage risk.

Value investing is a form of risk management

I was recently asked to present RBI to a large institutional money manager looking for new ideas. They listened to my ideas thoughtfully, asked good questions and eventually arrived at one question you would hope all money managers have on their minds, "What do you do to manage risk?"

I eventually discussed a number of risk management precautions I take but began with the simple assertion that one of the greatest things I do to manage risk is to systematically ensure I consider price before all else. The man who asked the question looked at me quizzically and said, "But risk is volatility, not price." His response is emblematic of Wall Street's preoccupation with models over logic and represents one edge you have against institutional investors.

Once again, Howard Marks is wise: "High risk, in other words, comes primarily with high prices... Whereas the theorist thinks return and risk are two separate things, albeit correlated, the value investor thinks of high risk and low prospective returns as nothing but two sides of the same coin, both stemming primarily from high prices."[153] There are two and only two ways to profit from the variability in stock prices. One is timing the market, which as you have seen is very hard to do. The other is by pricing, which is far easier to ascertain, if harder to stomach psychologically. The riskiness of an asset can never be divorced from the price that you pay for it; paying a fair price is the best friend of the risk-averse investor.

The idea that paying a fair price decreases risk makes sense intuitively, but also enjoys empirical support, even when playing by "their" rules that volatility equals risk. James O'Shaughnessy found in his mother-of-all-backtests that glamour stocks (i.e., high priced, analyst darlings) had higher standard deviations than their value stock (i.e., cheaply priced, despised by analysts) counterparts, a primary factor in the underperformance of the glamour names.

Tweedy, Browne LLC also demonstrate that value stocks fare better in hard times by measuring the performance of stocks by cheapness decile (as measured by price to free cash flow) in the worst 25 and 88 month periods. As you can see in table 5, there is a strong trend for less expensive stocks to lose less money during periods of market turbulence, a trend only bucked by the underperformance of the very cheapest decile of stocks (that were likely cheap for a reason).

Table 5—Average one-month investment returns (%) for stocks arranged by price-to-cash flow (PCF) in the worst and best stock market months, April 1968–April 1990[154]

PCF decile	Highest PCF ratio							Lowest PCF ratio		
	1	2	3	4	5	6	7	8	9	10
Return in worst 25 months for stock market (%)	−11.8	−11.1	−10.6	−10.3	−9.7	−9.5	−9.0	−8.7	−8.8	−9.8
Return in next worst 88 months when stock market declined (%)	−3.0	−2.8	−2.7	−2.4	−2.3	−2.1	−2.0	−1.9	−1.6	−2.0
Return in best 25 months for stock market (%)	12.1	12.5	12.2	11.9	11.6	10.9	11.2	11.5	11.9	13.6
Return in next best 122 months when stock market increased (%)	3.7	3.9	4.0	3.8	3.9	3.8	3.8	3.8	3.7	3.8

Finally, value stocks are not only prone to less loss in general, they are prone to less catastrophic loss, which is the far more damaging concern than general volatility. As Dr. Wesley Gray notes in *Quantitative Value*, "Glamour stocks were cut in half more than three times as often as value stocks; glamour stocks dropped 50% or more 7% of the time, while value stocks dropped 50% or more in approximately 2% of instances."[155] As Lakonishok, Vishny and Shleifer found in their

seminal paper 'Contrarian Investment, Extrapolation and Risk': "…
value strategies yield higher returns because these strategies exploit the
mistakes of the typical investor and not because these strategies are
fundamentally riskier."[156]

Medical students are famously asked to take the Hippocratic Oath,
a promise to uphold ethical standards that primarily revolves around
two concepts—non-maleficence and beneficence. Non-maleficence,
or the instruction to "First, do no harm," is the primary injunction
here and requires physicians to consider ways in which medical action
may actually harm the patient or introduce unforeseen risks. Although
it is more natural to consider beneficence—or actions that can be
undertaken for good—it is even more important to manage risk.
Likewise, the first and greatest task of an investor is to manage her
risks and paying a fair price is the single best way to do so.

But buying value stocks is not just a staid risk-management
technique. It has also been shown to increase returns across decades,
industries and continents, which is what we will explore next.

Finding 50 cent dollars

There are a number of ways to measure a stock's value, including price-
to-sales, price-to-earnings, price-to-book value and price-to-free cash
flow. While all of these measures have their strengths and weaknesses,
they all point to a fundamental truth—value stocks have outperformed
glamour stocks over long periods of time. James Montier found that
"star stocks" (i.e., those with good historic and forecast growth) were
outperformed by value stocks by nearly 6% per year.[157] Behavioral
economist Meir Statman found that "despised" stocks outperformed
glamour stocks even when accounting for variables used by critics to
poo-poo their performance, such as size, style and momentum.

Lakonishok, Vishny and Shleifer examined the effect of price-to-
book values on returns in 'Contrarian Investment, Extrapolation and
Risk'. They found that low price-to-book stocks (that is, value stocks)
outperformed the high price-to-book glamour stocks 73% of the time
over one-year periods, 90% of the time over three-year periods and

100% of the time over five-year periods.[158] They were so compelled by their research that they set up a highly successful investment firm based on its principles.

In 'Decile Portfolios of the NYSE, 1967–1985', Yale Professor Roger Ibbotson ranked stocks by deciles according to price-to-earnings ratios and measured their performance from 1967 to 1985. Ibbotson found that the stocks in the cheapest decile outperformed those in the most expensive decile by over 600% and the "average" decile by over 200% over that time period.[159] In a similar study, Eugene Fama and Kenneth French examined all non-financial stocks from 1963 to 1990 and divided them into deciles based on their price-to-book values. Over the period of their study, the least expensive stocks returned almost three times as much as the most expensive.[160]

One of the most exhaustive examinations of the various value factors was conducted by James O'Shaughnessy in his excellent read, *What Works on Wall Street*. O'Shaughnessy used the now-familiar methodology of dividing stocks into deciles and observing returns from 1963 to the end of 2009. His results highlight the efficacy of value investing and the power of slightly improved annualized returns to greatly compound wealth. Looking at price-to-earnings (P/E) ratios, he found that the cheapest decile of stocks with respect to P/E ratios turned $10,000 into $10,202,345 for a compound rate of return of 16.25% per year. Compare that to the index return of 11.22% that would have turned that same $10,000 into a mere $1,329,513. Buying cheap stocks would have made you $9,000,000 more and done so with less volatility, defying the efficient market notion that more risk is required for great returns.[161]

But what of the most expensive decile of stocks, the glamour names? The highest decile of P/E ratios turned $10,000 into $118,820 by 2009, over one million dollars less than the index and $10 million less than buying the despised value stocks. These numbers illustrate dramatically the words of Warren Buffett: "You pay a very high price in the stock market for a cheery consensus. Uncertainty is actually the friend of the buyer of long-term values."[162]

O'Shaughnessy's examination of other value variables yields similarly impressive results. The cheapest stocks as measured by enterprise value to EBITDA have outperformed the all stock index 100% of the time in rolling periods and by the wide margin of 181%. The most expensive stocks by that same measure have actually underperformed treasury bills! Inexpensive stocks as measured by price-to-free-cash-flow (P/FCF) have been similarly exceptional. The lowest decile of P/FCF stocks turned $10,000 in late 1963 into over $10 million by late 2009, far outperforming the index returns of $1.3 million over that same time period. Again, the performance was consistent as well, with cheap P/FCF stocks beating the index in 100% of rolling ten-year periods and 91% of rolling five-year periods.[163] I could go on, but I imagine my point has been well and truly proven by now. Value stocks tend to provide greater returns with lower volatility and incredible consistency—what's not to like?

Profitable pain

If value investing is such a slam dunk, then why is it that by some estimates, fewer than 10% of funds follow value principles?[164] In late 1997 at the height of the technology boom, an investor who put money into the most expensive decile of "story stocks" would have more than doubled his money by early 2000. This sort of massive compounding effect is largely the purview of growth stocks, which are by definition far more prone to this than their unsexy value counterparts. Value investing makes you rich over time, but growth investing can make you rich overnight.

However, as we learned earlier, there are no truer words on Earth than "this too shall pass." The same story stocks that made our fictional investor so wealthy over just over two years would have destroyed his wealth just as rapidly. Between February of 2000 and February of 2009, this highest decile of stocks would have dropped by 82%. Glamour investing has short-term upside but, as I have mentioned before, get rich quick and get poor quick are two sides of the same coin.

Research has shown that value investing has worked across time, continents and industries.[165] And while some investing anomalies are fleeting and trivial, I can say with some boldness that I believe value will serve long-term investors into the foreseeable future because of the way in which it interacts with human psychology. I bet on value investing for the same reasons that I'd bet on gyms to be more crowded in January than February. It's hard to stick with over time.

Value investing requires us to overcome our fundamental tendency to attribute greater quality to things that are more expensively priced. Value investing requires us to sacrifice short-term opportunities at fantastic wealth for longer-term consistency of returns. Being a value investor requires us to ignore the positive stories surrounding glamour stocks, hold our noses and buy shares of despised companies generally assumed to have poor prospects. Inasmuch as each and every one of these conditions is a direct violation of what comes naturally to most people, the value premium will continue to exist.

Joel Greenblatt of Magic Formula fame says that there really is no magic to the power of value investing. Instead, he suggests that you're just getting stocks with such low expectations that not even bad news can hurt them. Considering price first and foremost also means rooting your investment practices in the bedrock of reality rather than the air castles of forecast growth.

Glamour investing assumes that the future is knowable in ways that we have now seen it is not. Value investing deals with reality as it is presented and makes no assessments about the future other than that what goes up tends to go down and vice versa. You are programed in every way possible to pass on inexpensive stocks in favor of more expensive shares with better stories. Value investing requires you to deny your natural inclinations and do something that hurts. It's precisely because it's so painful that it pays so well.

What now?

Think—"Well bought is half sold."
Ask—"Would I buy the whole business at this price?"
Do—Systematically avoid expensive stocks. Yes, always.

2. Buy quality (PROPERTIES)

David Cook opened the first Blockbuster Video store in Dallas, Texas on February 6, 1963. Drawing on his expertise with managing huge databases, Cook was able to create systems where each Blockbuster store stocked videos that reflected the viewing preferences of the neighborhoods they served. On the strength of such mass customization, Blockbuster became a household name whose business practices were synonymous with innovation. In 1987, Blockbuster continued its inventive forward march, suing Nintendo to open the door to video game rentals.[166] Fast forward to the turn of the century and the now behemoth business was presented with an opportunity to buy upstart Netflix for $50 million. Blockbuster passed on the fledgling company in a meeting about which one Netflix co-founder said, "they just about laughed us out of their office."[167]

Later that year, Blockbuster moved in a different direction, deciding instead to sign with—of all companies—Enron Broadband Services. Today, Netflix, Inc. has a market cap of nearly $33 billion and Enron is, well, Enron. Over the early 2000s, Blockbuster stock was a rollercoaster as ideas about its relevance in a shifting digital landscape were still being formed. From the beginning of Q2 2012 to the end of Q4 2012, Blockbuster's stock price was cut in half, closing under $15. By many measures of "Price" discussed in the last section, Blockbuster was now an attractive bargain. But those investing on price-and-price-alone would have paid dearly for their unidimensionality. Five years later the stock price was just under $5 and ten years on the company no longer existed. A great American brand, founded and grown on innovation, was extinguished for a lack of the same.

This story illustrates that shares in a company can never be thought of as cheap or expensive based upon price alone, without carefully considering the quality of the company. After all, acknowledging that market participants are not wholly rational is a far different matter than suggesting that they are wholly irrational. Often times, a stock is cheap precisely because it is no good. In fact, Joseph Piotroski found that 57% of value stocks (as measured by price-to-book ratio) underperformed the market at one-and two-year intervals, even though they outperformed as a group. The reason that value strategies outperform is because a minority of value plays go on to show outsized positive performance in spite of the fact that market participants were right about most cheap stocks—they really did suck.

Imagine how well we could do if we could somehow sift through value stocks not only on price, but also on quality, getting all of the benefits of paying a fair price but also weeding out the stocks likely to underperform. The rule-based behavioral investor understands that price should always be conceived of relative to quality and seeks out not only good bargains, but good businesses.

Warren Buffett's mentor, Benjamin Graham, was a disciple of what Buffett refers to as "cigar butt investing". Graham hoped to pick discarded cigar butts of companies and take one last satisfying drag, even if they would eventually go bankrupt. Graham's "net-net" style of investing valued companies solely on their net current assets. He hoped to purchase companies for below their liquidation value so that even if they were eventually discarded (like a cigar butt), he could still profit from their misfortune.

Buffett began his career looking for these sort of net-net values, but soon realized they were becoming harder to find than when Graham was investing during the Great Depression. Buffett soon after partnered with Charlie Munger, who taught him the most important lesson of his investing life, that it is "far better to buy a wonderful company at a fair price than a fair company at a wonderful price."[168] We discussed paying a fair price in the previous section—now let's turn our attention to finding a wonderful company.

Beyond cigar butts

The combination of fair price and good company are some of the hallmarks of rule-based behavioral investing because they acknowledge the uncertainty of the future. We have no idea what the future will hold for the market or our chosen shares, so it is best to buy with some extra cushion with respect to both price and quality. In investing parlance, we are searching for a moat to fortify us against an unknowable tomorrow. No one describes this concept as nicely as LouAnn Lofton:

"Think of the idea of a moat just as you would the traditional fairy-tale moat around a castle, keeping a pretty long-haired girl protected from hungry dragons and lustful princes. A moat, in the business world, protects the company and its profit-making potential from hungry and lustful companies. It's anything that separates a company and gives it an advantage over its competition, resulting in higher profits for longer periods of time."[169]

It's an intuitive enough idea (after all, who wants to buy crummy businesses?), but it can be hard to look for a differentiator that accurately describes quality while still being predictive of improved future returns. One common mistake investors make when assessing the quality of a company is trying to determine whether or not the goods and services it provides will make important contributions to our lives, which is a different thing entirely than picking a sound investment. One of the things that makes good investing so difficult is that bad investing often begins with half truths, such as "revolutionary industries should make revolutionary money."

Consider the case of the airplane. It is hard to conceive of a technology that has had a greater impact on the way that we live and do business than the ability to quickly and cheaply fly relatively long distances. The National Air Traffic Controllers Association reports that there are over 87,000 flights per day in the US alone! And yet, investing in this marvelous, life-changing technology has almost always been a bad idea. Warren Buffett, an aviation enthusiast who has made some disastrous investments in airlines, put it very colorfully when speaking with the UK's *Telegraph* newspaper:

"If a capitalist had been present at Kitty Hawk back in the early 1900s, he should have shot Orville Wright. He would have saved his progeny money. But seriously, the airline business has been extraordinary. It has eaten up capital over the past century like almost no other business because people seem to keep coming back to it and putting fresh money in. You've got huge fixed costs, you've got strong labor unions and you've got commodity pricing. That is not a great recipe for success. I have an 800 (free call) number now that I call if I get the urge to buy an airline stock. I call at two in the morning and I say: 'My name is Warren and I'm an aeroholic.' And then they talk me down."[170]

Just like air travel, the internet has revolutionized our lives, but has not always provided investment returns to match. Internet users now send 204 million emails per minute, forever changing how we communicate. Facebook, with its goal to connect humanity, has passed the one billion user mark. Twitter now boasts over 370,000 tweets per minute and is powerful enough that a fake tweet erased $130 billion in value from the stock market in 2013.

There is no denying the unmitigated success of the internet, but like airplanes before them, internet stocks have often led investors to confuse societal impact with investment quality.

A Random Walk Down Wall Street describes how profit became passé during the internet bubble:

"Somehow in the brave new Internet world, sales, revenues, and profits were irrelevant. In order to value Internet companies, analysts looked instead at 'eyeballs'—the number of people viewing a Web page or 'visiting' a Web site. Particularly important were numbers of 'engaged shoppers'—those who spent at least three minutes on a Web site. Mary Meeker gushed enthusiastically about Drugstore.com because 48% of the eyeballs viewing the site were 'engaged shoppers.' No one cared whether the engaged shopper ever forked over any greenbacks. Sales were so old fashioned. Drugstore.com hit $67.50 during the height of the bubble of 2000. A year later, when eyeballs started looking at profits, it was a penny stock."

As Burton Malkiel wisely stated, "The key to investing is not how much an industry will affect society or even how much it will grow, but rather its ability to make and sustain profits."[171]

Are profits profitable?

If anticipating revolutionary new ideas won't put us on the road to riches, perhaps we should look at a more meat-and-potatoes metric of competitive advantage like profit margins. After all, wide profit margins seem like de facto evidence of a moat and are more sensible than non-financial metrics used to assess disruptive startups.

James O'Shaughnessy examined the effect of investing in the top decile of stocks by profit margin and compared these results to simply buying the all-stocks universe. If you had invested $10,000 in the top 10% of stocks with high profit margins every year beginning on December 31 of 1963, you would have ended with $911,179 by late 2009, a compound return of 10.31%. An impressive return, until you consider the do nothing alternative of buying the all stocks universe. An investment in that index would have yielded a return of 11.22% per year for a final balance of $1,329,513. By sensibly investing in the stocks with the best profits, you would have actually cost yourself over $400,000! These results corroborate those of Tweedy, Browne, which found that unprofitable cigar butt stocks outperformed their profitable cohorts by 2.4% per year.

What gives? If anticipating trends leads us to discount profits and looking at profits tends to underperform, where can we turn for quality? As with so much in investing, the failings of profit margin as evidence of quality have their roots in psychology.

Reflect on our earlier discussion of investment behavior, in particular our realization that excess is never permanent. It is human nature to project today's reality into the future unceasingly. If you are having a bad day today, it may seem as though the sun will never shine again. Similarly, we assume that the fortunes of a company will persist into the great forever despite the fact that just the opposite is true at the extremes. Companies with huge margins invite competitors to cut those margins down to size, to say nothing of the tendency for performance to mean-revert. When trying to determine the quality of a business it is best to remember that exceptional leaders tend to be followed by more mediocre replacements and that world-beating earnings seasons often sow the seeds for a less impressive future. In the words of Robert Frost:

Nature's first green is gold, Her hardest hue to hold.

Her early leaf's a flower; But only so an hour.

Then leaf subsides to leaf. So Eden sank to grief,

So dawn goes down to day. Nothing gold can stay.

The anecdotes shared above illustrate just how difficult investing can be and highlight the need for a systematic approach, since some parts of evidence-based investing frankly make no logical sense. "While it makes intuitive sense that stocks with great earnings gains and high profit margins should be good investments, the long-term data suggest otherwise. That's because successful investing relies heavily on buying stocks that have good prospects, but for which investors currently have low expectations." James O'Shaughnessy's words are telling: we must seek out hated companies whose prospects for the future are rising but are not yet obvious to The Crowd. It is easy enough to see if a stock is reviled. Its price relative to appropriate measures of value provides a great shorthand for investor expectations of future returns; the lower the price the more hated the shares. Assessing the future likelihood of coming back into favor is far trickier, but there are still clues.

Jason Zweig provides some such clues in his commentary on Ben Graham's masterwork, *The Intelligent Investor*:

"Several forces can widen a company's moat: a strong brand identity (think of Harley Davidson, whose buyers tattoo the company's logo onto their bodies); a monopoly or near-monopoly on the market; economies of scale, or the ability to supply huge amounts of goods or services cheaply (consider Gillette, which churns out razor blades by the billion); a unique intangible asset (think of Coca-Cola, whose secret formula for flavored syrup has no real physical value but maintains a priceless hold on consumers); a resistance to substitution (most businesses have no alternative to electricity, so utility companies are unlikely to be supplanted any time soon)."[172]

When you find a company that is both possessed of one of the aforementioned traits and selling at a discount, you may have stumbled on the all-important moat that is the hallmark of behavioral investing.

Of sheep and goats

An underappreciated hero of the value plus quality world, accounting professor Joseph Piotroski wanted to determine if he could separate wheat from chaff using accounting measures and created a simple metric that revolutionized value investing. In his own words:

> "success of that (value) strategy relies on the strong performance of a few firms, while tolerating the poor performance of many deteriorating companies. In particular, I document that less than 44% of all high BM (that is, inexpensive) firms earn positive market-adjusted returns in the two years following portfolio formation. Given the diverse outcomes realized within that portfolio, investors could benefit by discriminating, ex ante, between the eventual strong and weak companies. This paper asks whether a simple, financial statement–based heuristic, when applied to these out-of-favor stocks, can discriminate between firms with strong prospects and those with weak prospects."[173]

In plain English, how do we discern between cheap stocks that are cheap for a reason and good companies that are cheap for psychological reasons?

Professor Piotroski looked at nine measures of quality that later became referred to as a unit as the Piotroski F-score. The F-score considers profitability, leverage and operating efficiency to determine if a company is on firm financial footing in the present and, perhaps even more importantly, trending in a good direction. He awards one point for every positive indicator, for a maximum possible F-score of nine. The nine measures are as follows:

1. **Net income**—Is the bottom line positive?
2. **Operating cash flow**—Is trailing twelve-month operating cash flow positive?
3. **Return on assets (ROA)**—Has ROA improved year-over-year?
4. **Quality of earnings**—Does last year's operating income exceed ROA?
5. **Long-term debt vs. assets**—Is long-term debt decreasing relative to assets?

6. **Current ratio**—Is working capital increasing?
7. **Shares outstanding**—Have shares been diluted in the previous year?
8. **Gross margin**—Are margins increasing year-over-year?
9. **Asset turnover**—Are sales increasing relative to value of assets?

It is not essential for you to understand each of the component parts of the Piotroski F-score to benefit from its general usefulness. Piotroski set out to establish whether or not profitable companies that managed their debt, were good to their shareholders and operated efficiently would outperform their lower scoring peers and they did, handily. In 'Value Investing: The Use of Historical Financial Statement Information to Separate Winners from Losers', he demonstrated that a portfolio that bought the highest F-score companies (with scores of 8 or 9) and shorted the lowest F-score stocks (with scores of between 0 and 2) would have seen a 23% annualized return between 1976 and 1996.[174] The evidence suggests that if buying cheap stocks is good, buying high quality cheap stocks is much, much better.

Joel Greenblatt is another legendary investor who has created a name for himself by trying to systematize the Buffett-Munger approach of buying a wonderful company at a fair price. Greenblatt founded Gotham Capital in 1985 with a scant $7 million, put up primarily by junk-bond king Michael Milken.[175] Over the next 21 years, Greenblatt proceeded to put together one of the most impressive track records ever assembled on Wall Street by compounding his investors' wealth at 34% annualized en route to becoming a billionaire himself.[176] But something funny happened on the way to becoming super-rich; Greenblatt found that he could ring almost as much performance out of the market as he was with his complicated hedge fund by looking at just two variables.

Seeking to simplify value investing as much as possible, Greenblatt set out to create "a long-term investment strategy designed to help investors buy a group of above-average companies but only when they are available at below-average prices" by using just one variable to represent price and one other to represent quality. He settled on earnings yield (basically, the inverse of the price-to-earnings ratio) as his measure of value and return on capital (ROC) as his preferred measure of quality. Greenblatt's Magic Formula may sound simplistic, but the results it produced are anything but boring. The original Magic Formula included anything over $50 million in market cap and produced the remarkable backtested results shown in table 6.

Even when applied to larger cap companies (those with over $1 billion in market capitalization), the magic formula returned 19.7% per year from 1988 through 2009—a time period that included some very ugly volatility. Although he refers to it as a Magic Formula, there is no magic in Greenblatt's approach. He simply takes the intuitive, if underused, step of combining value with quality and the results speak for themselves. As with Piotroski, Greenblatt's measures work because they capture whether or not a company is using its resources wisely—that's it. A wise steward of resources selling at a bargain is almost always going to be good to its investors.

In business as in life, tough times are a matter of when and not if. As always, Warren Buffett put it more colourfully: "I try to buy stock in businesses that are so wonderful that an idiot can run them because sooner or later, one will." Whether the hardship is the result of an idiotic manager, an economic swoon or regulatory changes, the advice is the same—quality matters. Hardships are inevitable, comebacks are not, and quality is the best assurance you have that the market will one day find favor with your shares again.

Just as paying a fair price is an unrecognized risk management tool, assessing the quality of your purchase serves a similar function. Whether your chosen metric is brand equity, return on capital or operating efficiency, you should be able to say with some confidence that you have purchased a company worth owning well into the future. Ben Graham once opined that, "In the short run, the market is a voting machine but in the long run, it is a weighing machine." Price tells you how the market is voting for your shares at any given moment. Quality is your best guide to how they will eventually be weighed.

Table 6—Performance of Greenblatt's Magic Formula versus the S&P 500, 1988–2004[177]

	Magic Formula performance (%)	S&P 500 performance (%)
1988	27	17
1989	45	32
1990	2	-3
1991	71	31
1992	32	8
1993	17	10
1994	22	1
1995	34	38
1996	17	23
1997	40	33
1998	26	29
1999	53	21
2000	8	-9
2001	70	-12
2002	-4	-22
2003	80	29
2004	19	11

What now?

Think—"Quality is recognized over time."
Ask—"Is this a brand that can make its own rules?"
Do—Be prepared to pay a little more for quality.

3. Consider risk (PITFALLS)

"It's a racket. Those stock market guys are crooked."

—**Al Capone**

Gentle reader—although we've not likely had the opportunity to meet yet, I feel as though I know you. In fact, I feel like I know you well enough to make some suppositions about your personality. Let me give it a shot. Consider the following statements in terms of how true they are of you:

Although others may see you as put together, inside you can be worried and insecure. You want to be admired by others and you think about this when making decisions. Although you may not have done big things yet, you feel like that day will come. You feel as though you have a lot of untapped potential. You're an independent thinker who thoughtfully considers ideas before accepting them. You enjoy a certain amount of variety and change and dislike being held back by restrictions or limitations. You know you're not perfect, but you are typically able to use your personality strengths to compensate for your weaknesses.

So, how did I do? On a scale from 1 to 5, with 5 being the most accurate, how accurately would you say I described your personality? If you're like most people, you probably ranked that description of you as a 4 or 5, which likely puzzled you if we've never met.

The paragraph above illustrates what is called the Barnum Effect, or alternately the Fortune Cookie Effect. The Barnum Effect is named for P.T. Barnum, the great entertainer and circus magnate. Barnum famously posited that "There's a sucker born every minute" and used his knowledge of how to sucker people to get them to part with their money. Barnum's understanding of suckers, though born under the big top, undoubtedly surpasses that of many formally trained academicians. P.T. understood what psychologists call confirmation bias, or the human tendency to look for information that reinforces ideas we already hold.

When we receive feedback, there are two simultaneous dynamics that make up the broader phenomenon of confirmation bias. The first of these is self-verification, which is the tendency to reinforce existing beliefs. The second is self-enhancement, whereby we attend to information that makes us feel good about ourselves. The function of these two dynamics is clear—to maintain our self-esteem and feelings of confidence. In general, this is a positive; after all, who doesn't want to feel good about herself?

However, these dynamics work in overdrive in a number of instances—including when our deeply held beliefs or our self-esteem is challenged. Confirmation bias becomes problematic when it leads us to maintain the status quo in the face of disconfirmatory information or to overlook realistic, negative feedback about ourselves. In these instances, our need to feel competent can cause us to ignore warnings and take an overly rosy view of the future. That's all good and well you may say, but how does this impact my investment life? Well, far from being the rational *homo economicus* long-posited by efficient market theorists, your tendency to engage in confirmation bias is at least as pronounced when making financial decisions as it is in other aspects of your life. In fact, the high stakes and uncertain nature of financial decision-making is likely to lead you to engage in this fallacious thinking to an even greater degree.

Through one mechanism or another, you have formed opinions about how financial markets operate. Similarly, you have accumulated a portfolio of holdings, some of which you hold more dearly than others (e.g., the G.E. stock your deceased Aunt Bertha told you never to part with, rest her soul). For each of these holdings, there are myriad indicators that point to the relative health or sickness of the underlying assets but inasmuch as you want to maintain your view of yourself as competent and are loathe to stray from Bertha's words of wisdom, you will tend to emphasize the indicators that tell the story you want to hear.

The mark of a rule-based behavioral investor is that she is able to be a truth scientist—looking for information that both reinforces and flies in the face of her original hypothesis. Truth scientists understand that while "Why might this be a good investment?" is an OK question, a far superior question is "Why might I be wrong?"

If "Properties" is our indication that a stock could be of high quality, attending to "Pitfalls" helps us manage risk by ensuring that it is not of low quality. As Warren Buffett says, "An investor needs to do very few things right as long as he avoids big mistakes." But as you will see in our next story, considering the ways in which an investment might be a good idea comes far more naturally to humankind than an in-depth consideration of potential risks.

Look! Someone wrote "gullible" on the ceiling

Stephen Greenspan is a psychologist and author of the *Annals of Gullibility: Why We Get Duped and How to Avoid It*. Greenspan's book outlines notable instances of gullibility including the Trojan Horse, the failure to locate weapons of mass destruction in Iraq and the bad science surrounding cold fusion. Most of the book focuses on anecdotes, but the final chapter sets forth the anatomy of being fooled and attributes it to some combination of the following factors:

- **Social pressures**—Fraud is often committed within "affinity groups" such as people who hail from a similar religious background.
- **Cognition**—At some level, being duped represents a lack of knowledge or clarity of thought (but not necessarily a lack of intelligence).
- **Personality**—A propensity toward belief and difficulty saying "no" may lead people to be taken advantage of.
- **Emotion**—The prospect of some emotional payday (e.g., the thrill of making easy money) often catalyzes questionable decision-making.

In a field that is sorely understudied, Stephen Greenspan literally wrote the book on the topic. He is not just an expert on gullibility, he is *the* expert on gullibility. Which is why it may surprise you that he also lost 30% of his wealth to notorious fraudster Bernie Madoff.

In a candid assessment of his own gullibility, Greenspan wrote in *The Wall Street Journal*:

"In my own case, the decision to invest in the Rye fund reflected both my profound ignorance of finance, and my somewhat lazy unwillingness to remedy that ignorance. To get around my lack of financial knowledge and my lazy cognitive style around finance, I had come up with the heuristic (or mental shorthand) of identifying more financially knowledgeable advisers and trusting in their judgment and recommendations. This heuristic had worked for me in the past and I had no reason to doubt that it would work for me in this case.

The real mystery in the Madoff story is not how naive individual investors such as myself would think the investment safe, but how the risks and warning signs could have been ignored by so many financially knowledgeable people, including the highly compensated executives who ran the various feeder funds that kept the Madoff ship afloat. The partial answer is that Madoff's investment algorithm (along with other aspects of his organization) was a closely guarded secret that was difficult to penetrate, and it's also likely (as in all cases of gullibility) that strong affective and self-deception processes were at work. In other words, they had too good a thing going to entertain the idea that it might all be about to crumble."[178]

Greenspan has excellent insight into his own decision-making and motivation. He admits that he was relying on a shortcut ("Let other people think about it") that had worked in the past, without considering why it might not work this time around. Likewise, the professionals in the story had no interest in critically examining a system that was making them look like geniuses! As Francis Bacon said beautifully, "The human understanding when it once adopted an opinion draws all things else to support and agree with it. And though there be a great number and weight of instances to be found on the other side, yet these it either neglects and despises or else by some distinction sets aside and rejects; in order that by this great and pernicious predetermination the authority of its former conclusions may remain inviolate."

Just as Irvin Yalom found it difficult to entreat young lovers to think critically about the potential flaws in their relationship, it is nearly impossible to get someone who is making money to ask, "Why might I be wrong?"

"Speculation is an effort, probably unsuccessful, to turn a little money into a lot. Investment is an effort, which should be successful, to prevent a lot of money from becoming a little."[179] Fred Schwed's words illustrate a simple but profound concept: a systematic process for considering what might go wrong is what distinguishes investment from speculation. If risk management is the sine qua non of wise investing, why do we overlook it with such regularity?

The first answer is that risk is by its very nature invisible and present only in the future, making it frustrating to measure. Legendary money manager Howard Marks aptly compares risk-aware portfolio management to constructing buildings resistant to earthquakes. Until the ground starts shaking, no one appreciates (and may even complain about!) the extra time and money spent to insulate the building against future risks. As Marks observes, "It's much easier to sell 'Look what I did for you' than 'Look what I avoided for you.' I think most of you would agree that buying a car with seatbelts and airbags makes sense, even if you never plan on getting into a car wreck. Likewise, considering what could go wrong with potential investments is a sensible part of any paradigm, especially inasmuch as a 'crash' is virtually guaranteed for long-term investors."[180]

A second difficulty with risk management is that our flawed psychology leads us to subjectively experience low levels of risk when risk is actually quite high, a concept that Howard Marks refers to as the perversity of risk. While we tend to think of bear markets as risky, true risk actually builds up during periods of prosperity and simply materializes during bear markets. During good times, investors bid up risk assets, becoming less discerning and more willing to pay any price necessary to take the ride. Risks compound during such periods of bullishness, but this escalation goes largely undetected because everyone is making money. At some point, stocks become expensive, a risk ignored by most in the industry who equate risk directly with volatility.

Periods of dramatically positive returns increase interest in capital markets and bring about feelings of euphoria that lessen the perception of risk. All the while, rising valuations are increasing the risk of low returns down the road and bidding up prices to unsustainable levels. If you're relying on your gut rather than a rule-based approach to investing, you can be almost certain that your feelings of risk or safety are exactly the opposite of what they ought to be.

Risk may be invisible, but that is different from saying that it is impossible to guard against. As we saw in the first P of Price earlier, ensuring that we pay a fair price is one way to tilt both higher returns and lower risk in our favor.

A second concrete step that can be taken is to do what Berkshire Hathaway's Charlie Munger refers to as, "invert, always invert." When Munger encourages us to invert, he is telling us to consider the very question posed at the beginning of this chapter—"Why might I be wrong?" While this is a laudable exercise to consider individually, the idea that we can fully critically examine our own pet ideas with a truly objective eye ignores most of what we know about our own biases. As a result, a big part of my risk management efforts include enlisting the help of a dedicated Devil's advocate to help prod even the most Sacred Cow and question the assumptions of even the very favorite ideas. I do this myself. As this Devil's advocate, who I am paying to disagree with me, begins to shred my theses, I have to resist the very natural urge to try and argue against his or her points. In fact, the only questions I allow myself to ask are those dedicated to deepening my understanding of their contrarian hypothesis. I can ask, "Can you tell me more about why you think that way?" but assiduously avoid, "You're wrong and let me tell you why!"

Average investors will conduct a post-mortem on stocks that underperform, questioning after-the-fact what went wrong and seeking to apply those lessons learned to next time. But it is the mark of an exceptional investor to conduct a pre-mortem, imagining before the fact what might derail the hoped-for performance and making adjustments accordingly. As trader and psychologist Brett Steenbarger says of this concept, "Indeed, I have found that a large percentage of my winning trades begin with a rehearsal of negative, what-if scenarios in which I mentally invoke my stop strategy. Conversely, I have found that my worst trades begin with an estimate of my potential profits."[181]

Investment decision-making theorist Michael Mauboussin takes these concepts from the realm of the theoretical and has constructed a five-part checklist:

1. **Consider alternatives**—Decisions should never be made in a vacuum. Choices are only good or bad relative to the other options available to you. Ask: "What's my next best option?"
2. **Seek dissent**—Ask questions of others that are explicitly aimed at proving your views wrong. Shut up and take your medicine. Ask: "Where is my thinking off?"
3. **Keep track of previous decisions**—Write down why you are making a decision in the moment. Review those notes later to determine clarity of thought. Ask: "What mistakes have derailed past efforts?"
4. **Avoid making decisions while at emotional extremes**—Stress, fear, greed and excitement all color our perception of risk. Emotion is never absent from decision-making, but extreme emotions are antithetical to logic. Ask: "Am I emotionally in a place to be doing this?"
5. **Understand incentives**—Financial incentives are obvious drivers of investment decisions but other considerations come into play as well. Investors should be aware of reputational and career risk as the real motivators that they are. Ask: "What do I stand to gain or lose and how is that coloring my perception?"

Fool me once, shame on you

In addition to the typical considerations of business, market and behavioral risk, wise investors must also consider the sad but real existence of unscrupulous actors in the world of high finance. This lack of ethics can range anywhere from the legal-but-misleading world of accounting wizardry to the downright rotten tactics of the likes of Enron, all of which puts investors' capital at grave risk.

It is incumbent upon the behavioral investor then to consider the darker corners of human behavior and vet accordingly. Luckily for the less wonky among us, there are a number of helpful and underutilized tools for examining risks ranging from bankruptcy all the way to cooking the books. While a complete analysis of these ratios is beyond the scope of this book (and my attention span), I will highlight a couple of my favorites here, with an invitation for you to do further personal research if you wish.

Montier C-score

The "C" in C-score is for "cooking the books." This ratio was developed by investor and behavioral thinker James Montier to help identify short candidates, but can be just as useful in vetting longs. It looks at six parameters:

1. A growing difference between net income and cash flow from operations.
2. Increasing day's sales outstanding.
3. Growing day's sales of inventory.
4. Increasing other current assets relative to revenues.
5. Declines in depreciation relative to gross property, plant and equipment.
6. Serial acquisitions to distort earnings.

A stock receives one point for each of the conditions met with greater total points meaning a greater likelihood of book cooking. Montier found that stocks with high C-scores underperformed the US market by 8% per annum from 1993 to 2007. Combining the C-score with a measure of valuation provided even more powerful results. Stocks with both high C-scores and high valuations (as measured by a price-to-sales ratio of over 2) underperformed the market by 14%, with returns of negative 4% per annum. Accounting tricks may fool some in the short term but the long-term effects of such chicanery are disastrous for investors.

Altman Z-score

The Z-score is the brainchild of Edward Altman, a professor of finance at New York University at the time of his most important publication. The Z-score is Altman's (highly successful) effort at predicting which companies would go bankrupt within two years. In his backtest of 66 firms, Altman was able to correctly predict bankruptcy 72% of the time with a scant 6% of false positives. The Z-score is comprised of the following five components, weighted by their predictive power:

1. **Working capital/Total assets**—measures liquidity.
2. **Retained earnings/Total assets**—measures leverage.
3. **EBIT/Total assets**—measures profitability.
4. **Market cap/Total liabilities**—measures solvency.
5. **Sales/Total assets**—measures efficiency.

Altman's subsequent work has created a version of the formula to be used with private firms, although financial firms should not be examined with Z-scores given the complexity and opacity of their accounts. The Z-score's claim to fame is that it would have helped you avoid investing in Enron, which ultimately destroyed $60 billion of investors' wealth.

Risk and alternate endings

All too often we think of predicting the future as a necessary component of risk management. After all, if we could just polish that crystal ball a bit more, then maybe we'd have the knowledge necessary to prevent losses. But real-world risk management is less about a sure knowledge of the future than a deep understanding of the present. Risk may be invisible but it still casts a shadow.

The shadows of risk are apparent in stocks that are expensive relative to their fundamentals and companies that prefer manipulation to candor. The shadows of risk are present when we rely on our intuition over rules and value ego over honest critique. Risk management goes largely unheralded because it is amorphous, tedious and altogether less sexy than chasing returns. It is precisely for these reasons that it represents a great source of advantage to investors.

A blasphemous examination of one of baseball's most cherished moments will serve as a final punctuation on our look at risk. Backyard baseball heroes everywhere can recreate the scene all too well: an injury-hobbled Kirk Gibson, sick with a stomach virus, limp-running around second base and pumping his fist. Without a doubt, Gibby's home run is one of the most memorable in baseball history, setting up the Dodgers for an improbable Game One "W" and eventual World Series win. But in remembering the heroics of the moment, we tend to forget what came before.

The score at the time of Gibson's unexpected plate appearance was 4 to 3 in favor of the Oakland Athletics, whose mulleted (and we now know, steroid-fueled) superstar Jose Canseco had hit a grand slam in the first inning. Canseco had an outstanding year in 1988, hitting .307 with 42 homeruns, 124 RBIs and, eye-popping by today's standards, 40 stolen bases. Loading the bases in front of Canseco in the first inning was massively risky, as was throwing him the hanging slider that he eventually parked over the center field fence. But riskier still was sending Gibson to bat sick with the flu and hobbled by injuries sustained in the NLCS (the previous round of matches). That we don't perceive it as risky is an example of what psychologists call counterfactual thinking. It turned out in the Dodgers' favor, so their manager Tommy Lasorda is viewed as a strategic genius. But had it not, and simple statistics tell us that getting a hit is never in even the best hitter's favor, Lasorda would have been a goat.

Just as we laud improbable and memorable athletic achievements without adequately accounting for risk and counterfactuals, we do likewise with large and singular financial events: Paulson's shorting of subprime mortgage products; Soros shorting $10 billion in currency. These events are so large, so memorable and worked out so favorably that we ascribe to them a level of prescience that may not correspond with the expected level of risk-adjusted return.

A friend of mine once joked that, "every man thinks he is ten sit-ups away from being Brad Pitt." Having observed significant overconfidence among both professionals and novice traders alike, I might similarly assert that "every stock market enthusiast thinks that he is one trade away from being George Soros." It's fun to talk about The Greatest Trade of All Time, but most real wealth is accumulated by not striking out rather than hitting dramatic home runs. If a consistent, detailed look at potential pitfalls is not currently a part of your investment discipline you are overlooking the surest path to winning—namely, not losing.

What now?

Think—"Over the long term, I win by not losing."
Ask—"Is there evidence of fraud and manipulation, or are results too-good-to-be-true?"
Do—Utilize C-scores, Z-scores, M-scores and skepticism to vet all purchases.

4. Follow the leaders (PEOPLE)

"Jesus Christ said, 'by their fruits ye shall know them,' not by their disclaimers."

—**William S. Burroughs**

You have now spent a fair amount of time considering what it takes to become a behavioral investor and are long overdue for some action and intrigue. Let's imagine briefly that instead of being the psychologically savvy investor you are quickly becoming, you are the Army's chief interrogator. You have apprehended a bad guy who is now tied to a chair in a dank interrogation room, illuminated by a single swaying light bulb.

He is rumored to have placed a bomb in a major metropolitan area but you can't be certain if this is bluster or a credible threat. You have a sense of where the bomb might be placed if one exists, but it's Christmas in Megacity, USA and the presence of a bomb squad will scare the holiday shoppers and be an embarrassment to your department if it's a false alarm. You have a choice—you can either spend the time to determine whether or not your prisoner is lying (no, you cannot use "enhanced interrogation techniques") or you can risk unnecessary dramatics and send in the bomb squad immediately. The choice relies on one fundamental question—can you spot a liar?

Television shows like Lie to Me have popularized the notion that experts can detect dissimulation simply by tuning into microexpressions—that is brief, involuntary facial expressions that show the true underlying motivations of potential deceivers. But, to my great dismay as a fan of the show, the research tells another story. The US Transportation Security Administration (TSA), hoping to prevent another 9/11-type disaster, has spent over $1 billion training thousands of behavior detection officers to scan crowds of passengers for nonverbal clues that would give away a potential terrorist. The usefulness of such a program seems logical enough and the motivation is certainly laudable but the results have been disappointing to say the least. A review by the Government Accountability Office recommended axing the program altogether because there was no proof of effectiveness.[182]

This decision is buttressed by a meta-analysis of 200 studies of body language deception detection by Charles F. Bond, Jr. and Bella M. DePaulo.[183] In their exhaustive examination of the literature, Bond and DePaulo found that people correctly identified liars at a worse rate than chance (47%)! You would be better off flipping a coin to determine whether or not someone is lying than trying to conduct an in-depth analysis of their behavior. As psychologist Maria Hartwig says of this phenomenon, "The common-sense notion that liars betray themselves through body language appears to be little more than a cultural fiction."[184]

A 2005 paper by Kassin, Meissner and Norwick goes even further to disprove the idea that experts can read body language. The three researchers enlisted the help of prisoners serving time and asked them to record a confession of the crime they committed as well as one fictional crime. They then asked a group of students as well as a group of trained law enforcement professionals to view the confessions and determine the real crimes from the made-up stories. The professionals were no lightweights—with an average experience of 11 years and a majority having received deception detection training, one would guess that they could outperform a group of students credentialed only in watching CSI while drinking cheap beer.

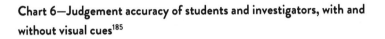

Chart 6—Judgement accuracy of students and investigators, with and without visual cues[185]

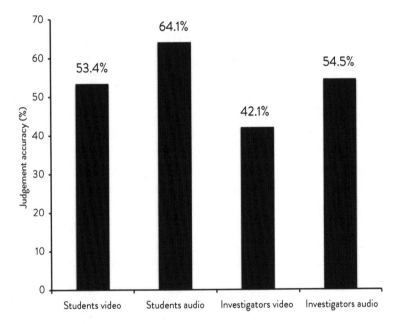

Once again, expertise proves to increase confidence but not performance. Students were able to accurately judge the video statements as true or false 53.4% of the time, despite expressing limited confidence in their abilities (6.18/10). Experts, on the other hand, were far more confident (7.65/10) but also much worse at divining the truth. For all of their training and experience, law enforcement experts were once again worse than a coin flip, correctly discerning honesty a scant 42% of the time. Interestingly, taking body language cues away served to dramatically enhance the predictive power of both groups (see results in chart 6). The research suggests that not only is body language not predictive of greater insight, but it actually distracts us from finding the truth!

The seven habits of highly defective people

Across hundreds of peer-reviewed studies, it is becoming abundantly clear that we are not great (okay, really not even all right) at detecting who is being honest. Despite this overwhelming evidence, however, fund managers continue to waste their clients' money on fundamental deep dives into the quality and character of the management of potential investment targets.

We want very badly to believe that there should be some advantage in meeting with management face-to-face, having lunch with them and examining the cut of their jib, so to speak. It is an understandable human tendency to hope that we can judge character and by extension the prospects of a company, by meeting the people responsible for its success. Unfortunately, it's a trick of the mind and a colossal waste of time and money.

Sydney Finkelstein's book *Why Smart Executives Fail* purports to be a checklist for spotting corporate leaders destined to run their companies into the ground.[186] While the typical business book fawns over the positive traits of business leaders, Finkelstein took the opposite tack and tried to identify the "derailers" common to the disastrous leader. My own summary of his sort of Seven Habits of Highly Defective Managers is as follows:

1. They see themselves and their companies as dominating their environments.
2. They identify so completely with the company that all boundaries between their personal interests and those of the company are blurred.
3. They seem to have all the answers.
4. They ruthlessly eliminate anyone not on board with their vision.
5. They are consummate company spokespeople and devote a great deal of time to maintaining the company's image.
6. They treat intimidating obstacles as temporary impediments to be dispatched.
7. They are quick to return to the old strategies that made them effective in the first place.

Drawing on dramatic examples like WorldCom, Tyco and AOL/Time Warner, Finkelstein makes a compelling case for something we'd all like to believe—tyrants make bad bosses.

Although Finkelstein's book was not written until 2004, let's pretend for a moment that you had access to such a checklist on April 1, 1976, the day that Apple Inc. was formed. Imagine that you, the intrepid analyst for MegaFund, LP are charged with evaluating the leadership skills of one Steve Jobs relative to the seven criteria you see above. This is the same Steve Jobs who singled out and fired employees in company-wide meetings. The same man who denied his child love and financial support for years in spite of a positive paternity test. The very same Steve Jobs whose idea of recruiting was telling a competitor at Xerox, "Everything you've ever done in your life is shit, so why don't you come work for me?"

Undoubtedly, you would have left your meeting with Jobs determined that he was brilliant, but using Finkelstein's ideas would have led to a dim view of his leadership abilities. Likely, you would have passed on the investment based on your gut-level instincts about what makes a good leader and the presence of every single one of the seven measures above. You also would have forfeited a 31,590% return on investment from your meeting until July of 2015.

Everyone thinks their baby is beautiful

Every quarter, the prestigious Duke University Fuqua School of Business and *CFO Magazine* team up to conduct a survey of CFOs and magazine subscribers. The survey is constant over time in an effort to "capture trend data on corporate optimism, expected GDP growth, capital investment plans, and quarterly percentage changes in a variety of business categories."[187]

A consistent finding of the survey, pointed out by James Montier in his white paper 'Seven Sins of Fund Management: A Behavioural Critique', is that CFOs generally have a higher opinion of their own companies than the economy at large. In examining the Duke survey data, Graham and Harvey found that almost 90% of tech CFOs thought their stock was undervalued near the peak of the tech bubble.[188] Everyone thinks their baby—and their business—is more beautiful than all of the others, no matter how statistically impossible that is.

It is a natural and worthwhile impulse to want firsthand insights into how a business is run before making an investment, it just turns out that in-person meetings are an ineffective way of arriving at that information. To begin with, analysts and fund managers have a built-in bias for the result of the meeting to be positive. After all, if the management being scrutinized is disappointing, the trip and all of the time invested were for naught. Do you know how expensive it is to fuel a private jet?!

A second problem is management's unrealistically rosy outlook on their business relative to the broader business environment. As a result of this overconfidence, you can be confident that management is misleading you even if they are not aware that they are! Finally, we have a worse-than-chance ability of telling if someone is being honest with us. In-person due diligence of management, for all its common sense appeal, is really little more than an expensive boondoggle that gives fund managers false confidence while passing the considerable expenses on to their clients.

The idea that we should be examining the behavior of the people inside a business remains a good one, even if the means by which we have gone about it are flawed. The good news is that there is much we can glean about those running a business, and none of it requires a tedious steak dinner or an insufferable dog and pony show with no basis in fact. There are three types of information that give us valuable insight about the people inside a business and help us to weigh up the investment case of that business: share buybacks, insider trades and dividends.

Symptoms don't lie

House, M.D. is an American TV series that enjoyed eight successful seasons from 2004 to 2012. Dr. House, the show's main character, is a pill-popping misanthrope played to perfection by Hugh Laurie. The show is enjoyable in spite of being highly formulaic, with each episode revolving around some hard-to-diagnose malady that Dr. House inevitably divines by ignoring the obfuscation of the patient in favor of focusing on their symptoms. As Dr. House was wont to say, "Patients lie but symptoms don't."

Insider trades

The same can be said about management behavior and there is no truer guide to how they feel about their business than the way they spend their money. Corporate insiders are appropriately mandated to disclose the buying and selling of their own shares and these insider trades can give strong behavioral insights to the watchful investor. Indeed, the trades of corporate insiders beat the market by six percentage points each year, bested only by the trades of senators (who are allowed to trade on their privileged information), who outperform by a whopping 12% per annum.[189]

When someone with intimate knowledge of a business's prospects is willing to vote with her own money, you should take note. There are plenty of reasons for insiders to sell a stock (e.g., house in the Hamptons, divorce settlement, hush money for their mistress) but there is only one good reason to buy—a well-informed faith in a brighter tomorrow.

Giamouridis, Liodakis and Moniz present evidence that the positives of insider buying cross borders in their paper, 'Some Insiders are Indeed Smart Investors'.[190] The authors found that in the UK, the larger the absolute value of the insider trade, the more dramatic the subsequent returns. They also found what you might have already guessed; the knowledge possessed by the insider today comes to be understood by the market over time. Insider purchases outpace the market by 0.7% immediately after the purchase but the size of the outperformance grows to 2.9% by day 120.

Tweedy, Browne Company, in their seminal, 'What Has Worked in Investing: Studies of Investment Approaches and Characteristics Associated with Exceptional Returns', examined the returns of stocks with significant insider buying action.

Specifically, they included only studies in which more than one insider had purchased a company's shares and the number of insider purchases had exceeded the number of insider sales over the time period in question. The findings of these insider buying studies show that buying stocks heavily favored by insiders gets you anywhere from almost two times to four times the average result of the index over a similar time period! Their results can be seen in table 7.

Table 7—Investment returns after insiders' purchases[191]

Study author	Study period	Annualized investment return (%)	
		Insider stocks	Market index
Rogoff	1958	49.6	29.7
Glass	1961–1965	21.2	9.5
Devere	1960–1965	24.3	6.1
Jaffe	1962–1965	14.7	7.3
Zweig	1974–1976	45.8	15.3

The results of these studies are so dramatic that they make me wonder, "Why would I ever listen to what management says about their stock when the answer is right in front of me?" There is no truer gauge of what a person thinks or values than how they spend their money.

Share buybacks

In addition to insider buying, management can also evince optimism for the future by tapping the corporate coffers to buy back shares of their own stock. Warren Buffett describes this pithily:

> "One usage of retained earnings we often greet with special enthusiasm when practiced by companies in which we have an investment interest is repurchase of their own shares. The reasoning is simple: if a fine business is selling in the market place for far less than intrinsic value, what more certain or more profitable utilization of capital can there be than significant enlargement of the interests of all owners at that bargain price? The competitive nature of corporate acquisition activity almost guarantees the payment of a full price—frequently more than full price when a company buys the entire ownership of another enterprise. But the auction nature of security markets often allows finely-run companies the opportunity to purchase portions of their own businesses at a price under 50% of that needed to acquire the same earning power through the negotiated acquisition of another enterprise."[192]

Buying back shares is evidence that the company is bullish on their future and also has the fortunate side effect of increasing your percentage ownership of the firm. Given this combination of positive future expectations and immediate payoff, it's no wonder that the returns to companies that aggressively buy back shares are so good. A 1985 Fortune article by Carol Loomis looked at the investment returns of companies that had aggressively bought back shares of their own stock from 1974 to 1983.[193] Assuming that investments were made on the date of repurchase and held until 1984, the companies that bought back shares averaged a 22.6% compounded annual return versus 14.1% for the S&P 500.

James O'Shaughnessy also examined buyback outperformance in *What Works on Wall Street*. O'Shaughnessy created a metric he refers to as "buyback yield", which compares the number of stocks outstanding from one period to another to distinguish true buybacks from the sneaky practice of simultaneously buying back stock and issuing new shares. He found that companies with the highest buyback yield (i.e., those who reduced the number of outstanding shares the most) averaged 13.69% next year returns compared to a measly 5.94% average return for the lowest decile of buyback yield (i.e., those who increased the number of outstanding shares the most).

One common critique is that the act of announcing a share buyback can be a crafty PR move rather than an actual intention on the part of the company. But as Dr. Wes Gray suggests in *Quantitative Value*, "The mere announcement of a buyback is often enough to move a stock up. Stocks announcing a buyback—whether they follow through with the buyback or not—outperform immediately following the announcement and over the longer term."[194] Share buybacks are so powerful that even their very mention has an outsized positive effect on performance.

Dividends

Insider trades and share buybacks lead to outperformance because they give us undiluted insights into what people in the know think about a business. Just as important as how management acts is how they treat you, the shareholder. As surely as nothing says "I believe in this business" like buying back shares, nothing says "I love my shareholders" like an appropriate dividend. If buying a stock is partial ownership of a business, receiving a dividend means getting back a portion of the profits.

Depending on whom you ask, dividends have accounted for between 44% and just over 50% of historical stock returns,[195] but stocks with generous dividends are often derided as being "widow and orphan" stocks (i.e., safe, non-cyclical stocks with limited upside). The psychological reasons for devaluing something as remunerative as a nice dividend are complex, but as you are now aware, learning to find great value that is greatly overlooked is the heart of rule-based behavioral investing.

One reason to love dividends is that, although they are not guaranteed, they tend to fluctuate less than the stock market itself.

As Ben Carlson points out, "Between September 1929 and June of 1932, the stock market fell 81% as measured by the inflation-adjusted S&P index. But in that time inflation-adjusted dividends only fell 11%. When the market fell 54%, from January of 1973 to December of 1974, real dividends fell only 6%."[196] If dividends are nice to have in good times, they are essential in bad times.

We should also consider that dividends are far from just a defensive play; they can also dramatically enhance returns if understood correctly. James O'Shaughnessy divided stocks into deciles by dividend yield and returned fascinating results—his research suggests that dividends are powerful and yet there can be too much of a good thing. The highest decile of dividend yielding stocks from 1926 to 2009 returned a handsome 11.77% annualized, solidly outperforming the broader universe of stocks at 10.46% a year. However, the top decile was actually outperformed by the stocks in the second, third and fourth deciles—those with solid-but-safe dividends. Investing in the third decile, the most productive of the lot, would have turned $10,000 into an incredible $145 million over the time period studied.

Stocks with eye-popping dividends may be trying to lure in yield-seeking investors with the "guarantee" of easy money. Sadly, the gaudy yield may be hiding deeper problems, which accounts for the lack of outperformance. Investors in stocks with no dividend, on the other hand, are betting almost exclusively on the growth of the share price, which is a gamble that doesn't always go the shareholders' way. Stocks that pay adequate dividends reward the shareholders today without mortgaging the future with excessive payouts.

As I'm sure you're beginning to notice, the behavioral investing themes that I've identified in the US market also tend to work internationally. Human nature abides (just like The Dude) and the tendency to make predictably irrational money moves is one that unites the entire human family. Consistent with this theme, a study conducted by Professor Mario Levis of the University of Bath examined performance relative to dividend yield of 4413 companies listed on the London Stock Exchange from 1955 to 1988.[197]

The results are presented in table 8, where once again, we see a strong, nearly linear, relationship between dividend yield and investment returns. Unlike O'Shaughnessy's analysis, Levis finds that the only exception to the "more-dividends-more-return" rule are stocks that pay no dividend at all tend to have slightly better than market performance (albeit far below the performance of even the top 50% of stocks that do pay a dividend).

Table 8—Investment results of UK companies according to dividend yields, 1955–1988[198]

Dividend yield group	Yield (%)	Annual investment return (%)	Dec 1988 value of £1m starting investment (£m)	Average market cap (£m)
1	13.6	19.3	403.4	283.4
2	10.9	17.7	254.9	278.5
3	8.7	16.8	196.4	337.2
4	7.4	16.0	155.4	266.4
5	6.4	15.4	130.3	223.1
6	5.5	14.1	88.7	206.5
7	4.7	12.4	53.2	112.1
8	4.0	11.9	45.7	95.4
9	3.1	11.5	40.5	94.4
10	1.4	13.8	81.1	74.6
FT All-Share Index	5.3	13.0	63.8	503.5

Your actions speak so loud I can't hear a word you're saying

Behavioral investing is rooted in the idea that people are central to all aspects of the investment process, but part of that means realizing our own limitations. Hedge fund and mutual fund managers love to talk about putting "boots on the ground" and "really digging in" with management, but this tends to be nothing more than a confirmation bias lovefest that wastes client money on efforts that have intuitive appeal but little real efficacy.

Instead of paying high fees for a fund manager to lob softball questions at a CEO, examine the truest compass of their intentions—their behavior. Are they spending their own hard-earned money to buy back shares because they believe in the business? Are they using the company money to purchase shares they believe to be attractively priced? Do they care enough about you to let you share in the profits? If so, you might have a winning investment idea. If not, you are likely confronted with leadership that cares more about lining their own pockets than filling yours. As James W. Frick noted, "Don't tell me where your priorities are. Show me where you spend your money and I'll tell you what they are."

What now?

Think—"Who knows better than the people inside the business?"
Ask—Don't ask. Just see what those in the business are doing with their money and do likewise.
Do—Only become a partial owner of a company that loves you back.

5. Go with the flow (PUSH)

"Every trend goes on forever, until it ends."

—**John Neff**

Being the person of exquisite taste and incomparably good looks that you are, I am certain that you have never lacked for love. But for means of scientific exploration, let us imagine a fictional alternate reality where you are single, lonely and in search of The One. Picture further that you are approached by a well-meaning friend who does what such friends do and sets you up on a blind date with an acquaintance of theirs, who we'll refer to as The Friend. You feign struggle and disinterest at first ("I'm fine. Really!") but persuaded by the cobwebs on your tandem bicycle, you ultimately relent.

You meet The Friend and are immediately glad you disregarded your "no setups" rule. The Friend is attractive, kind and an excellent conversationalist. The Friend gets you into a restaurant with a six-month waiting list, speaks at length about philanthropic efforts and evinces a snarky-but-not-cynical wit that you find endearing. As the first date ends you already find yourself looking forward to the next—could this finally be The One?

Your second date is a dance lesson that provides you much longed-for closeness, the third is a picnic lunch in Central Park and your fourth date finds you at the opera house. You pretend to enjoy opera so as not to appear a rube (the only thing that has kept opera alive for centuries). Yes, four dates in and you are really starting to fall for The Friend. And then it all takes a turn for the worse. Date number five begins with The Friend picking you up in a Yugo instead of the luxury sedan you had become accustomed to. Not wishing to be rude, you make no mention of the conspicuous downgrade. The Friend's casual couture has also been replaced by wrinkled clothing soiled with what appears to be a mustard stain (please be a mustard stain, please be a mustard stain).

Worst of all, The Friend's demeanor has changed entirely. The once-lovable wit has turned bitter and mean and is sometimes pointed in your direction. Generosity of spirit has given way to pettiness and lofty discussion of ideas has been usurped by gossiping about your mutual friends. At the end of the fifth date (at a bowling alley) your head is spinning. You must now decide if you should go on a sixth date but are unsure of whether Jekyll or Hyde will greet you at the door. The Friend needs an answer—think seriously about what you would decide to do.

If you are like most people (and you are, regardless of your answer to this question), you decide to give The Friend a sixth date and a second chance. The reasons for your largesse can be found not in your big heart, but in the psychological principles of anchoring and confirmation bias. Anchoring refers to the all-too-human tendency to rely on the first piece of information when forming opinions and making decisions.

When you meet someone new you begin forming opinions of them within seconds. This tendency is best summed up in the dandruff shampoo slogan, "You never get a second chance to make a first impression." These first impressions, or anchors, then set the guardrails within which future impressions tend to fall. All new information is processed relative to your initial anchor and your snap judgments about the type of person you are interacting with. Confirmation bias, on the other hand, is the tendency to interpret new information in a way that is consistent with our preconceptions and our best interests.

In the case of The Friend, you had early positive interactions that led you to conceptualize this person as intelligent, sophisticated, funny and kind. Additionally, you have personal reasons for wanting them to be all of those things because sleeping alone at night is no fun! Not only did you observe The Friend to be a good person, you actually *need* The Friend to be a good person so that you don't have to die alone surrounded by your cats.

This potent combination of anchoring and confirmation bias leads us to project today's reality far into the future and to underreact to new information. In life, that gives us wasted time dating a bum. In finance, that gives us momentum, or push, as we refer to it here. Just as we assume a desirable date will be desirable going forward, we tend to project a stock's current prospects out into the future. Momentum effects are undeniably irrational; the vestiges of a brain equipped for parsimony over probability. They are also undeniably powerful.

A (very) brief history of momentum investing

The idea of momentum began with and still draws much of its language from the world of physics. It is essentially a financial extrapolation of Newton's first law of motion: every object in a state of uniform motion tends to remain in that state of motion.[199] As Corey Hoffstein of Newfound Research puts it, "Momentum is a system of investing that buys and sells based upon recent returns. Momentum investors buy outperforming securities and avoid—or sell short—underperforming ones... They assume outperforming securities will continue to perform in absence of significant headwinds."[200]

Digging a little deeper, there are actually two types of momentum: absolute and relative. Absolute momentum compares a stock's recent performance to its own historical performance, whereas relative momentum examines the moves of a security relative to other securities. Both rely on a similar maxim: strength and weakness persist over the short term.

I will provide a truncated history of momentum research below; those interested in a more comprehensive take should read the work of Gary Antonacci (*Dual Momentum Investing*) and Corey Hoffstein ('Two Centuries of Momentum' white paper). Although viewed by some value investing purists as voodoo, momentum actually has a two-century-long history of empirical support.

As early as 1838, James Grant published a volume that examined the wildly successful trading strategy of English economist David Ricardo. Grant says of Ricardo's success:

"As I have mentioned the name of Mr. Ricardo, I may observe that he amassed his immense fortune by a scrupulous attention to what he called his own three golden rules, the observance of which he used to press on his private friends. These were, 'Never refuse an option when you can get it,'—'Cut short your losses,'—

'Let your profits run on.' By cutting short one's losses, Mr. Ricardo meant that when a member had made a purchase of stock, and prices were falling, he ought to resell immediately. And by letting one's profits run on he meant, that when a member possessed stock, and prices were raising, he ought not to sell until prices had reached their highest, and were beginning again to fall. These are, indeed, golden rules, and may be applied with advantage to innumerable other transactions than those connected with the Stock Exchange."[201]

Although it had been practiced ad hoc for years, the first rigorous empirical examination of momentum was produced by Herbert Jones and Alfred Cowles III in 1937. Jones and Cowles found that from 1920 to 1935, "taking one year as the unit of measurement... the tendency is very pronounced for stocks which have exceeded the median in one year to exceed it also in the year following."[202]

By the 1950s, investment newsletter author George Chestnutt had this to say of momentum strategies:

"Which is the best policy? To buy a strong stock that is leading the advance, or to shop around for a sleeper or behind-the-market stock in the hope that it will catch up? On the basis of statistics covering thousands of individual examples, the answer is very clear as to where the best probabilities lie. Many more times than not, it is better to buy the leaders and leave the laggards alone. In the market, as in many other phases of life, the strong get stronger, and the weak get weaker."[203]

A contemporary of Chestnutt, Nicolas Darvas introduced "BOX theory", wherein he bought stocks reaching new highs (i.e., having broken out of their old box) and hedged his bets with tight stop losses. Said Darvas of his methods, "I keep out in a bear market and leave such exceptional stocks to those who don't mind risking their money against the market trend."[204] Then Robert Levy introduced the concept of relative strength in the late 1960s, but following his efforts momentum went largely ignored for nearly three decades.

As the fundamental investing approach of Benjamin Graham (and later Warren Buffett) began to take hold, momentum was increasingly seen as a form of near-charlatanism. Buffett himself minces no words when discussing his distaste for price momentum: "I always find it extraordinary that so many studies are made of price and volume behavior, the stuff of chartists. Can you imagine buying an entire business simply because the price of the business had been marked up substantially last week and the week before?"[205]

In more recent years, momentum has seen an increase in acceptance among theorists, because whatever mortal quirks may drive its presence, its persistence and pervasiveness are undeniable. In 'Returns to Buying Winners and Selling Losers: Implications for Stock Market Efficiency' by Jegadeesh and Titman, we see that from 1965 through 1989, winning stocks continued to outperform losing stocks on average over the next six to 12 months. And the size of the outperformance was sizeable—1% per month, even after adjusting for return differences owing to other risk factors.[206]

Indeed, the effects of momentum tend to be pervasive and not limited with respect to market, place or time. Chris Geczy and Mikhail Samonov conducted what is affectionately referred to as "the world's longest backtest" and found that momentum effects have persisted in the US since 1801![207] Momentum signals have worked well in the UK since the Victorian Age[208] and have proven their power and persistence across 40 countries and more than a dozen asset classes![209] So deep-seated are our psychological tendencies toward momentum that, "the momentum premium has been a part of markets since their very existence, well before researchers studied them as a science." As with all financial variables that spring from unconscious psychological proclivities, it seems reasonable to postulate that momentum is here to stay.

Momentum plus...

By now you may find yourself at the same crossroads I did when I first became convinced of the power of momentum. We have both intuitive and empirical evidence of its existence on the one hand, but on the other hand, who are we to disagree with Warren Buffett? A more nuanced look tells us that both the "momentum is great" and "momentum is voodoo" camps have valid points and that by taking the best of both worlds we can access the power of push with less downside than a pure momentum strategy.

James O'Shaughnessy examined the performance of the decile of stocks with the best six-month momentum against the all stocks universe and found that the momentum strategy compounded wealth at 14.11% versus 10.46% for the broader market.[210] While three or so percentage points might not sound dramatic, it was the difference between a final portfolio value of nearly $573 million for momentum and not quite $39 million for the all stock holdings (with a $10,000 initial investment on December 31, 1926). O'Shaughnessy also found that momentum outperformed with some consistency, beating the benchmark 87% of the time in rolling five-year periods.[211]

It's settled then! We'll just buy the top 10% of momentum stocks each year and retire with a Scrooge McDuck-esque pile of gold coins, right? Not so fast. Although momentum in isolation is usually a great bet, when it goes wrong it can go very wrong. As you might have already guessed, some momentum stocks will be expensive. They are trending more expensive after all. This being the case, pursuing a pure momentum strategy can get you crushed at the top of speculative bubbles like the Tech Wreck of the turn of the century. In the run up to the bubble bursting, momentum excelled, with the top decile soaring 42.24% from December of 1995 to February of 2000.[212] However, the exact opposite occurred over the next three years, with high-momentum stocks going on to lose nearly half of their value—far worse than the market at large.

What if rather than pursuing a pure push strategy, we combined it with what we already know about paying a fair price? In 'The Interaction of Value and Momentum Strategies', Cliff Asness examines the power of combining these two empirically sound investment strategies.[213] Not surprisingly, he finds that price and push are negatively correlated, meaning that cheap stocks tend not to have momentum and momentum stocks tend not to be cheap. By dividing stocks into quintiles based on their expensiveness and momentum, Asness was able to compare the results of the worst of both worlds (high price, low momentum) with the best of both worlds (low price, high momentum) and his results were remarkable. He found that the high price, low push portfolios returned a disappointing 0.36% annualized against an impressive 19.44% annualized for the low price, high push baskets. If combining momentum with fundamentals is voodoo, hand me a needle and a doll.

As James O'Shaughnessy has correctly noted, "of all the beliefs on Wall Street, price momentum makes efficient market theorists howl the loudest." In a perfect world, there would be no good reason to pay more for a business today than yesterday simply because of positive price action. But this isn't a perfect world, it's Wall Street Bizarro World and these are the rules.

When Benjamin Graham introduced cigar butt investing he set forth the simple but unchangeable truth that the price you pay for a business matters a great deal. Charlie Munger built upon this foundation by encouraging Warren Buffett to buy great companies at a fair price. Behavioral investing is the next iteration of this proud legacy and recognizes that paying a fair price for a good business is maximally rewarding when others begin to agree with your assessment.

Five Ps summary

There are a number of sound ways to invest in a rule-based behavioral manner, the five Ps presented here being but one example. The five Ps work because they are research-based, simple and measure the fundaments of a business. It makes both common and empirical sense that buying high quality, inexpensive companies that are playing by the rules and have the faith of management should outperform.

You may be able to improve upon the five P model by adding your own factors to an RBI framework, but it won't be by dreaming up something esoteric. Rule-based behavioral investing works for the simple reason that doing little things that have a big impact over long periods of time yields incredible results.

What now?

Think—"A stock in motion tends to stay in motion."

Ask—"How has this done on a relative and absolute basis over the last six months to one year?"

Do—Automate a process of buying a concentrated basket of attractively priced, high-quality companies that are enjoying a recent catalyst.

Epilogue. Behavioral Investing In A World Gone Mad

"You don't become a value investor for the group hugs."

—Seth Klarman

EDWIN LEFÈVRE WAS a Colombian-born journalist, writer and diplomat who is most remembered for his writings on the culture of Wall Street. Although he wrote eight books, he is most celebrated for *Reminiscences of a Stock Operator,* an ostensibly fictional account that most suppose to be a thinly veiled biography of Jesse Livermore. My favorite passage from Lefèvre's magnum opus is a memorable take on the extraordinary distance between theory and application in investing:

"I have heard of people who amuse themselves conducting imaginary operations in the stock market to prove with imaginary dollars how right they are. Sometimes these ghost gamblers make millions. It is very easy to be a plunger that way. It is like the old story of the man who was going to fight a duel the next day.

His second asked him, 'Are you a good shot?'

'Well,' said the duelist, 'I can snap the stem of a wineglass at twenty paces,' and he looked modest.

'That's all very well,' said the unimpressed second. 'But can you snap the stem of the wineglass while the wineglass is pointing a loaded pistol straight at your heart?' "

To this point, this book has asked little of you. You have read what is required of you behaviorally to manage yourself and your money. Having internalized the wisdom of the great market thinkers I have compiled here, you are now theoretically skilled enough to shoot down behavioral inefficiencies from 20 paces. The only problem is, the market shoots back.

I have sought to disseminate knowledge about the impact of behavior on everything from managing risk to personal decision-making to individual security selection. In some endeavors, this sort of book learning is necessary and sufficient to be successful. But in investing, knowledge alone always lacks.

Emanuel Derman cites the ideas of Friedrich Hayek, the Austrian economist and Nobel laureate on the differences between hard sciences and softer pursuits like investment management. Derman asserts, "in the physical sciences we know the macroscopic through concrete experience and proceed to the microscopic through abstraction."[214] For example, the earliest theories dealt with ideas immediately accessible to our senses (e.g., pressure) that eventually led us to an understanding that pressure is the work of microscopic atoms. In the hard sciences, macro observations have tended to pave the way for theorizing and exploration on a micro level.

Given to profound "physics envy" (like all of the social sciences are—yes, investing is a social science), early attempts at "scientizing" investment management began with the big picture and largely ignored individual market participants. It is precisely for this reason that they got it wrong. As Derman says, "the order of abstraction should be reversed: we know the individual agents and players from concrete personal experience and the macroscopic 'economy' is the abstraction. If the correct way to proceed is from concrete to abstract ... in economics we should begin with agents and proceed to economics and markets rather than vice versa."[215]

The psychology of individuals—warts and all—must be a central consideration in the formulation of any practical investing approach. The good news here is that others' misbehavior will consistently and systematically create opportunities for you. The bad news is that you are prone to all of the same quirks and are just as likely, in the absence of strict adherence to the rules, to create the same opportunities for others.

This fact—that we are all prone to systematic errors in thinking and acting—is the answer to the excellent question, "Why should any of this work going forward?" After all, you're hardly the only one with access to research on the power of considering ideas like Price, People and Push. But I can say with some confidence that the power of these ideas will persist for the very same reason that I can say with some confidence that people will always overeat, cheat on their spouses and fear sharks more than Big Macs. America is not a fat nation because we are short on gyms or nutritional information. We are fat because donuts taste better than broccoli. Hedge fund manager Seth Klarman endorsed this idea when he said:

"So if the entire country became securities analysts, memorized Benjamin Graham's *Intelligent Investor* and regularly attended Warren Buffett's annual shareholder meetings, most people would, nevertheless, find themselves irresistibly drawn to hot initial public offerings, momentum strategies and investment fads. People would still find it tempting to day-trade and perform technical analysis of stock charts. A country of security analysts would still overreact. In short, even the best-trained investors would make the same mistakes that investors have been making forever, and for the same immutable reason—that they cannot help it."[216]

The fact that people are fallible is your biggest enduring advantage in the accumulation of greater wealth. The fact that you are just as fallible is the biggest impediment to that very same goal.

If human inconsistency is one reason why an RBI approach will continue to enjoy success over the long-term, a second reason is less intuitive. Namely, it's precisely because it can be a short-term failure. There will be months and even years in which the approach will be outperformed by any variety of other approaches. Warren Buffett has "lost his touch" more times than I can count. Joel Greenblatt's Magic Formula, which has crushed the performance of the S&P 500 over the medium and long term, has underperformed the market for as long as three years consecutively and has historically underperformed in five out of every 12 months.

During such times, short-sighted investors will question the efficacy of the RBI model, ignore its simple wisdom and abandon ship. If history is any teacher, these exits will likely be followed by periods of outperformance shortly thereafter. As Benjamin Graham observed "It would be rather strange if—with all the brains at work professionally in the stock market—there could be approaches which are both sound and relatively unpopular. Yet our own career and reputation have been based on this unlikely fact."[217]

It has correctly been suggested by many of the greatest investors that behavioral investing is a lonely pursuit that is not undertaken by those concerned about popularity contests. Long before the term behavioural finance was ever coined, John Maynard Keynes, made this observation:

"It is the long-term investor, he who most promotes the public interest, who will in practice come in for the most criticism, wherever investment funds are managed by committees or boards or banks. For it is in the essence of his behavior that he should be eccentric, unconventional and rash in the eyes of average opinion. If he is successful, that will only confirm the general belief in his rashness; and if in the short run he is unsuccessful, which is very likely, he will not receive much mercy. Worldly wisdom teaches that it is better for reputation to fail conventionally than to succeed unconventionally."[218]

Rule-based behavioral investing is precisely what Keynes predicted the crowd would misunderstand—an unconventional path to success. Some of your friends, staunch indexers for instance, will find the RBI approach too active for their taste. Others, those who insist on making large bets on a single stock, will find your patient, systematic approach too staid. But a truism in money management as elsewhere in life is that a steady, middle way will lead to satisfying results, no matter how unconventional it may seem in the moment.

To this point we have considered myriad advantages to behavioral investing but have overlooked the greatest boon of all—the incalculable benefit of introspection and personal growth. From the outside looking in, most people suppose investing to be a wholly sterile affair, bereft of humanity and concerned only with the pursuit of profit. But as truly competent investors deepen their understanding of the human element of investing, they are presented not only with opportunities to improve processes but also to improve lives. Jason Zweig said the following in an impassioned speech to investment professionals:

"You will do a great disservice to yourselves, to your clients, and to your businesses, if you view behavioral finance mainly as a window onto the world. In truth, it is also a mirror that you must hold up to yourselves. More worrisome, it is a mirror that magnifies and clarifies and highlights your own warts and imperfections.

After all, it takes no great bravery to look out a window onto the world below and watch the foolish masses aimlessly stumbling nowhere near where they really want to go—while you can see quite clearly, from your lofty vantage point, the simplest and safest path to follow.

But it takes a great deal of courage to stare into a mirror and to hold it steady for a long, long time while this image sinks in: Gazing right back at you is someone who relentlessly falls prey to the law of small numbers; to hindsight bias; to over-reaction; to narrow framing; to mental accounting; to status-quo bias; to the inability to evaluate your own future regret; and, most of all, to overconfidence."[219]

The Ancient Greeks believed in geocentricity, the now-implausible notion that the Earth is the center of the Universe, around which all others objects orbit. In classical antiquity, it was widely supposed that the body contained four humors, blood, black bile, yellow bile and phlegm, and that optimal health resulted from an appropriate balance of the four. In the not-too-distant past, doctors applied leeches to "let" the blood of the infirm, supposing that this was the key to vibrancy. In an effort to maintain personal and professional humility, I keep a phrenology skull in my office, a reminder of the practice of making inferences about someone's character and personality based on the contours of their head. Scarier still, there is inevitably something that we believe today that will seem just as preposterous to future generations.

Much as we laugh at such anachronism today, I am certain that the time is not far distant that we will wonder that we ever developed financial models that did not somehow seek to account for the behavior of market participants. I have three young children and it is my fervent hope that there will be no behavioral finance courses offered when they attend college. If there are, we will still be mired in the same intellectual turf wars that can keep great ideas from exploring their points of fusion rather than their surface dissimilarities. Instead, I hope they will learn about finance as a complicated, tentative, somewhat messy discipline that their professors will approach with some mathematical precision, but would never dream of disconnecting from the people that give it life. Integrating psychology and finance provides for the possibility of increasing both our returns and our awareness of self—therein lies true wealth.

Bibliography

Antonacci, G., *Dual Momentum Investing: An Innovative Strategy for Higher Returns with Lower Risk* (McGraw-Hill Education, 2014)

Ariely, D., *Predictably Irrational: The Hidden Forces that Shape Our Decisions* (HarperCollins, 2009)

Arnott, R. D., Berkin, A.L. and Ye, J., 'How Well Have Taxable Investors Been Served in the 1980's and 1990's?', *First Quadrant* (2000)

Arnott, R. D., Hsu, J.C. and West, J.M., *The Fundamental Index: A Better Way to Invest* (John Wiley & Sons, 2008)

Asness, C. S., 'The Interaction of Value and Momentum Strategies', *Financial Analysts Journal* 53:2 (1997)

Asness, C. S., Frazzini, A., Israel, R. and Moskowitz, T.J., 'Fact, Fiction and Momentum Investing' (SSRN, 2014)

Asness, C. S., Ilmanen, A. and Maloney, T., 'Market Timing Is Back In The Hunt For Investors' institutionalinvestor.com (November 11, 2015)

Bennyhoff, D. G. and Kinniry Jr., F.M., 'Advisor's alpha', Vanguard.com (April, 2013)

Bernstein, P., *Against The Gods: The Remarkable Story of Risk* (John Wiley & Sons, 2008)

Blanchett, D. and Kaplan, P., 'Alpha, Beta, and Now... Gamma', Morningstar (August 28, 2013)

Bond, Jr., C. F. and DePaulo, B.M., 'Accuracy of Deception Judgments', *Personality and Social Psychology Review* 10:3 (2006)

Brown, J. M., *Backstage Wall Street: An Insider's Guide to Knowing Who to Trust, Who to Run From, and How to Maximize Your Investments* (McGraw-Hill Education, 2012)

Browne, C. H., Browne, W. H., Spears, J. D., Shrager, T. H. and Wyckoff, Jr., R. Q., 'What Has Worked In Investing: Studies of Investment Approaches and Characteristics Associated with Exceptional Returns' (Tweedy, Browne Company, 1992)

Browne, C. H., 'Value Investing and Behavioral Finance', presentation to Columbia Business School (November 15, 2000)

Browne, C. H., *The Little Book of Value Investing* (John Wiley & Sons, 2006)

Browne, C. H., Browne, W. H., Spears, J. D., Shrager, T. H. and Wyckoff, Jr., R. Q., 'What Has Worked In Investing: Studies of Investment Approaches and Characteristics Associated with Exceptional Returns' (Tweedy, Browne Company, revised edition, 2009)

Buffett, W. E., 'The Superinvestors of Graham-And-Doddsville' (1984)

Carlson, B., *A Wealth of Common Sense: Why Simplicity Trumps Complexity in Any Investment Plan* (John Wiley & Sons, 2015)

Casselman, B., 'Worried About The Stock Market? Whatever You Do, Don't Sell.', FiveThirtyEight.com (August 25, 2015)

Chabot, B., Ghysels, E. and Jagannathan, R., 'Momentum Cycles and Limits to Arbitrage—Evidence from Victorian England and Post-Depression US Stock Markets' (NBER working paper, 2009)

Cialdini, R. B., *Influence: The Psychology of Persuasion* (Harper Business, 2006)

Cogliati, G. M., Paleari, S. and Vismara, S., 'IPO Pricing: Growth Rates Implied in Offer Prices' (SSRN, February 1, 2008)

Cohen, R. B., Polk, C. and Silli, B., 'Best Ideas', SSRN.com (March 15, 2010)

Connors, R. J., *Warren Buffett on Business: Principles from the Sage of Omaha* (Wiley, 2009)

Cremers, M. and Petajisto, A., 'How Active is Your Fund Manager? A New Measure That Predicts Performance' (SSRN, March 31, 2009)

Damodaran, A., Damodaran Online, Investment Management, 'Risk and Time Horizon'.

Davies, G. B. and de Servigny, A., *Behavioral Investment Management: An Efficient Alternative to Modern Portfolio Theory* (McGraw-Hill Education, 2012)

DePodesta, P., 'Draft Review—About Process', itmightbedangerous. blogspot.com (June 10, 2008)

Derman, E., *Models.Behaving.Badly.: Why Confusing Illusion with Reality Can Lead to Disaster, on Wall Street and in Life* (Free Press, 2012)

Diamond, J., *Collapse: How Societies Choose To Fail Or Succeed* (Viking, 2005)

Dinkelman, T., Levinsohn, J. A. and Majelantle, R., 'When Knowledge Isn't Enough: HIV/AIDS Information and Risk Behavior in Botswana', NBER Working paper (2006)

Evans, J. L. and Archer, S. H., 'Diversification and the Reduction of Dispersion: An Empirical Analysis', *The Journal of Finance* 23:5 (December 1968)

Faber, M. T., 'A Quantitative Approach to Tactical Asset Allocation' (SSRN, February 1, 2013)

Fama, E., French, K. R., 'The Cross-Section of Expected Stock Returns', *Journal of Finance* 47:2 (1992)

Felder, J., 'Don't Buy The Buy-And-Hold Line Of BS', thefelderreport. com (August 5, 2014)

Felder, J., 'How To Time The Market Like Warren Buffett: Part 1', thefelderreport.com (August 7, 2014)

Felder, J., 'Are Passive Investors Taking On Far More Risk Than They Realize?', thefelderreport.com (February 3, 2016)

Finkelstein, S., *Why Smart Executives Fail: And What You Can Learn from Their Mistakes* (Portfolio, 2004)

Galbraith, J. K., *A Short History of Financial Euphoria* (Penguin, 1994)

Geczy, C. and Samonov, M., 'Two Centuries of Price Return Momentum' (SSRN, 2016)

Giamouridis, D., Liodakis, M. and Moniz, A., 'Some Insiders are Indeed Smart Investors' (SSRN, July 29, 2008)

Gilbert, D., 'The surprising science of happiness', TED.com (February 2004)

Goldstein, N. J., Martin, S.J. and Cialdini, R.B., *Yes!: 50 Scientifically Proven Ways to Be Persuasive* (Free Press, 2009)

Graham, J. R. and Harvey, C. R., 'Expectations, optimism and overconfidence' (2005)

Graham, B. and Zweig, J., *The Intelligent Investor: The Definitive Book on Value Investing. A Book of Practical Counsel* (Harper Business, 2006)

Graser, M., 'Epic Fail: How Blockbuster Could Have Owned Netflix', *Variety* (November 12, 2013)

Gray, W. R., and Carlisle, T., *Quantitative Value: A Practitioner's Guide to Automating Intelligent Investment and Eliminating Behavioral Errors* (John Wiley & Sons, 2012)

Gray, W. R., Vogel, J. R. and Foulke, D. P., *DIY Financial Advisor: A Simple Solution to Build and Protect Your Wealth* (John Wiley & Sons, 2015)

Greenblatt, J., *You Can Be a Stock Market Genius: Uncover the Secret Hiding Places of Stock Market Profits* (Touchstone, 1999)

Greenblatt, J., *The Little Book That Still Beats the Market* (John Wiley & Sons, 2010)

Greenspan, S., 'Why We Keep Falling for Financial Scams', *The Wall Street Journal* (January 3, 2009)

Grenny, J., Patterson, K., Maxfield, D., McMillan, R. and Switzler, A., *Influencer: The Power to Change Anything* (McGraw-Hill Education, 2013)

Griffin, T., 'A Dozen Things I've Learned from Marty Whitman/Third Avenue about Investing', 25iq.com (December 15, 2013)

Hargreaves, R., 'Seth Klarman: Now's Not The Time To Give Up On Value', valuewalk.com (January 26, 2016)

Housel, M., '25 Important Things to Remember As an Investor', fool.com (March 28, 2013)

Howard, C. T., *Behavioral Portfolio Management: How successful investors master their emotions and build superior portfolios* (Harriman House, 2014)

Howard, C. T., *The New Value Investing: How to Apply Behavioral Finance to Stock Valuation Techniques and Build a Winning Portfolio* (Harriman House, 2015)

Ibbotson, R., 'Decile Portfolios of the NYSE, 1967–1984', Yale School of Management Working Paper (1986)

Jegadeesh, N. and Titman, S., 'Returns to Buying Winners and Selling Losers: Implications for Stock Market Efficiency', *Journal of Finance* 48:1 (1993)

Jones, M. A., *Women of The Street: Why Female Money Managers Generate Higher Returns (and How You Can Too)* (Palgrave Macmillan, 2015)

Kalchik, B., 'Top 10 Cases Of The SI Cover Jinx', rantsports.com (October 7, 2014)

Keynes, J. M., *The General Theory Of Employment, Interest, And Money* (CreateSpace, 2011)

Lakonishok, J., Vishny, R.W. and Shleifer, A., 'Contrarian Investment, Extrapolation and Risk' (Working paper, 1993)

Lincoln, A., 'Address before the Wisconsin State Agricultural Society', abrahamlincolnonline.org (September 30, 1859)

Lindstrom, M., *Buyology: Truth and Lies About Why We Buy* (Random House Business, 2009)

Lofton, L., *Warren Buffett Invests Like a Girl: And Why You Should, Too* (Harper Business, 2012)

Loomis, C. J., 'Beating the market by buying back stock', *Fortune* (November 21, 2012)

Malkiel, B.G. and Ellis, C., *The Elements of Investing: Easy Lessons for Every Investor* (John Wiley & Sons, 2013)

Malkiel, B. G., *A Random Walk Down Wall Street: The Time-Tested Strategy for Successful Investing* (W. W. Norton & Company, 11th edition, 2016)

Marks, H., *The Most Important Thing: Uncommon Sense for the Thoughtful Investor* (Columbia University Press, 2011)

Mauboussin, M. J., *Think Twice: Harnessing the Power of Counterintuition* (Harvard Business Review Press, 2012)

Max, S., 'Writing a Bigger Book', *Barron's* (August 23, 2014)

Montier, J., 'Seven Sins of Fund Management: A behavioural critique', DrKW Macro Research (November 2005)

Montier, J., 'Painting by numbers: an ode to quant', DrKW Macro Research (August 2, 2006)

Montier, J., *Value Investing: Tools and Techniques for Intelligent Investment* (John Wiley & Sons, 2009)

Montier, J., *The Little Book of Behavioral Investing: How not to be your own worst enemy* (John Wiley & Sons, 2010)

O'Shaughnessy, J., *What Works on Wall Street: The Classic Guide to the Best-Performing Investment Strategies of All Time* (McGraw-Hill Education, 4th edition, 2011)

Peters, T. J. and Waterman, Jr., R. H., *In Search of Excellence: Lessons from America's Best-Run Companies* (Harper Business, 2006)

Piotroski, J. D., 'Value Investing: The Use of Historical Financial Statement Information to Separate Winners from Losers', University of Chicago Graduate School of Business (2002)

Portnoy, B., *The Investor's Paradox: The Power of Simplicity in a World of Overwhelming Choice* (St Martin's Press, 2014)

Rayer, M. D., 'Goals-Based Investing Saves Investors from Rash Decisions', SEI Wealth Network (2008)

Reed, T., 'Buffett Decries Airline Investing Even Though at Worst He Broke Even', *Forbes* (May 13, 2013)

Schwartz, B., *The Paradox of Choice: Why More Is Less* (Harper Perennial, 2005)

Shiv, B., 'Thinking Money—Horizontal Wine Tasting', YouTube.com (October 14, 2014)

Silver, N., *The Signal and the Noise: Why So Many Predictions Fail—but Some Don't* (Penguin, 2015)

Soe, A.M., 'SPIVA U.S. Scorecard', S&P Dow Jones Indices (2014)

Statman, M., *What Investors Really Want: Know What Drives Investor Behavior and Make Smarter Financial Decisions* (McGraw-Hill Education, 2010)

Steenbarger, B. N., *The Psychology of Trading: Tools and Techniques for Minding the Markets* (John Wiley & Sons, 2002)

Taleb, N. N., *Fooled By Randomness: The Hidden Role of Chance in Life and in the Markets* (Random House, 2005)

Taleb, N. N., *Antifragile: Things That Gain from Disorder* (Random House, 2014)

Task, A., 'Pride cometh before the fall: Indexing edition', aarontask. tumblr. com (August 29, 2014)

Tetlock, P., 'Theory-Driven Reasoning about Plausible Pasts and Probable Futures in World Politics' in *Heuristics and Biases: The Psychology of Intuitive Judgment*, ed. T. Gilovich, D. Griffen, and D. Kahneman (Cambridge University Press, 2003)

Tierney, J., 'At Airports, a Misplaced Faith in Body Language', *The New York Times* (March 23, 2014)

Widger, C. and Crosby, D., *Personal Benchmark: Integrating Behavioral Finance and Investment Management* (John Wiley & Sons, 2014)

Yanofsky, D., 'How you could have turned $1,000 into billions of dollars by perfectly trading the S&P 500 this year', qz.com (December 16, 2013)

Zweig, J., 'Behavioral Finance: What Good Is It, Anyway?', jasonzweig. com (June 20, 2015)

Endnotes

1   J. Grenny, K. Patterson, D. Maxfield, R. McMillan and A. Switzler, *Influencer: The Power to Change Anything* (McGraw-Hill Education, 2013), p. 17.

2   S. Fiorillo, 'What Is the Average Income in the U.S.?', TheStreet (February 11, 2020).

3   Damodaran Online, Investment Management, 'Risk and Time Horizon'.

4   N. Silver, *The Signal and the Noise: Why So Many Predictions Fail—but Some Don't* (Penguin, 2015).

5   B. Carlson, *A Wealth of Common Sense: Why Simplicity Trumps Complexity in Any Investment Plan* (John Wiley & Sons, 2015), p. 12.

6   M. Statman, *What Investors Really Want: Know What Drives Investor Behavior and Make Smarter Financial Decisions* (McGraw-Hill Education, 2010), p. 6.

7   L. Lofton, *Warren Buffett Invests Like a Girl: And Why You Should, Too* (Harper Business, 2012), p. 25.

8   J. Diamond, *Collapse: How Societies Choose To Fail Or Succeed* (Viking, 2005).

9   G. Antonacci, *Dual Momentum Investing: An Innovative Strategy for Higher Returns with Lower Risk* (McGraw-Hill Education, 2014), p. 83.

10   B. Graham and J. Zweig, *The Intelligent Investor: The Definitive Book on Value Investing. A Book of Practical Counsel* (Harper Business, 2006), p. 215.

11   D. G. Bennyhoff and F. M. Kinniry Jr., 'Advisor's alpha', Vanguard. com (April, 2013).

12   D. Blanchett and P. Kaplan, 'Alpha, Beta, and Now… Gamma', Morningstar (August 28, 2013).

13   'The Value Of Financial Planning', Financial Planning Standards Council, fpsc.ca.

14   J. M. Brown, *Backstage Wall Street: An Insider's Guide to Knowing Who to Trust, Who to Run From, and How to Maximize Your Investments* (McGraw-Hill Education, 2012), p. 9.

15   Graham and Zweig, *Intelligent Investor*, p. 217.

16   Carlson, *Common Sense*, p. 68.

17   Ibid, p. 26.

18   N. J. Goldstein, S. J. Martin and R. B. Cialdini, *Yes!: 50 Scientifically Proven Ways to Be Persuasive* (Free Press, 2009), p. 188.

19   J.K. Galbraith, *A Short History of Financial Euphoria* (Penguin, 1994), p. 6.

20   D. Ariely, *Predictably Irrational: The Hidden Forces that Shape Our Decisions* (HarperCollins, 2009), p. 97.

21   Ibid.

22   B. N. Steenbarger, *The Psychology of Trading: Tools and Techniques for Minding the Markets* (John Wiley & Sons, 2002), p. 54.

23   G. M. Cogliati, S. Paleari and S. Vismara, 'IPO Pricing: Growth Rates Implied in Offer Prices' (SSRN, February 1, 2008).

24   M. Lindstrom, *Buyology: Truth and Lies About Why We Buy* (Random House Business, 2009), pp. 27–28.

25   J. O'Shaughnessy, *What Works on Wall Street: The Classic Guide to the Best-Performing Investment Strategies of All Time* (McGraw-Hill Education, 4th edition, 2011), p. 26.

26   J. Montier, *Value Investing: Tools and Techniques for Intelligent Investment* (John Wiley & Sons, 2009).

27   T.J. Peters and R.H. Waterman, Jr., *In Search of Excellence: Lessons from America's Best-Run Companies* (Harper Business, 2006).

28   Brown, *Backstage Wall Street*, p. 6.

29   Montier, *Value Investing*, p. 17.

30   Galbraith, *A Short History*, p. 110.

31   Lindstrom, *Buyology*, p. 54.

32   Ibid.

33   R. B. Cialdini, *Influence: The Psychology of Persuasion* (Harper Business, 2006), p. 115.

34   Ibid., p. 118.

35   Ibid.

36   Graham and Zweig, *Intelligent Investor*, p. 219.

37   M. D. Rayer, 'Goals-Based Investing Saves Investors from Rash Decisions', SEI Wealth Network (2008).

38   C. Widger and D. Crosby, *Personal Benchmark: Integrating Behavioral Finance and Investment Management* (John Wiley & Sons, 2014), p. 158.

39   Ibid., p. 159.

40   Grenny, Patterson, Maxfield, McMillan and Switzler, *Influencer*, p. 89.

41   D. Gilbert, 'The surprising science of happiness', TED.com (February 2004).

42   N. N. Taleb, *Antifragile: Things That Gain from Disorder* (Random House, 2014), p. 150.

43   Montier, *Value Investing*, p. 11.

44   O'Shaughnessy, *What Works on Wall Street*, p. 11.

45   Graham and Zweig, *The Intelligent Investor*, p. 374.

46   C. H. Browne, *The Little Book of Value Investing* (John Wiley & Sons, 2006).

47   B. G. Malkiel, *A Random Walk Down Wall Street: The Time-Tested Strategy for Successful Investing* (W. W. Norton & Company, 11th edition, 2016), p. 167.

48   B. Portnoy, *The Investor's Paradox: The Power of Simplicity in a World of Overwhelming Choice* (St Martin's Press, 2014), p. 36.

49   P. Tetlock, 'Theory-Driven Reasoning about Plausible Pasts and Probable Futures in World Politics' in *Heuristics and Biases: The Psychology of Intuitive Judgment*, ed. T. Gilovich, D. Griffen, and D. Kahneman (Cambridge University Press, 2003).

50   Brown, *Backstage Wall Street*, p. 148.

51   J. Montier, *The Little Book of Behavioral Investing: How not to be your own worst enemy* (John Wiley & Sons, 2010), p. 78.

52   J. Greenblatt, *The Little Book That Still Beats the Market* (John Wiley & Sons, 2010), p. 30.

53   Ibid, p. 102.

54   Carlson, *Common Sense*, p. 52.

55   Graham and Zweig, *The Intelligent Investor*, p. 260.

56   A. Lincoln, 'Address before the Wisconsin State Agricultural Society', abrahamlincolnonline.org (September 30, 1859).

57   B. Kalchik, 'Top 10 Cases Of The SI Cover Jinx', rantsports.com (October 7, 2014).

58   P. Bernstein, *Against The Gods: The Remarkable Story of Risk* (John Wiley & Sons, 2008), p. 271.

59   O'Shaughnessy, *What Works on Wall Street*, p. 21.

60   Montier, *Value Investing*, p. 95.

61   Ibid., p. 205.

62   Carlson, *Common Sense*, p. 22.

63   O'Shaughnessy, *What Works on Wall Street*, p. 28.

64   Ibid., p. 30

65   Graham and Zweig, *The Intelligent Investor*, p. 16.

66   H. Marks, *The Most Important Thing: Uncommon Sense for the Thoughtful Investor* (Columbia University Press, 2011), p. 100.

67   Carlson, *Common Sense*, p. 126.

68   Ibid., p. 72.

69   Ibid., p. 133.

70   Antonacci, *Dual Momentum*, p. 51.

71   Ibid., p. 56.

72   Ibid., p. 56.

73   Marks, *The Most Important Thing*, p. 36.

74   Graham and Zweig, *The Intelligent Investor*, p. 122.

75   M. Housel, '25 Important Things to Remember As an Investor', fool.com (March 28, 2013).

76   'Historical Returns for US Stock/Bond Allocations, And Choosing Your Allocation', QVM Group (July 30, 2013).

77   G. B. Davies and A. de Servigny, *Behavioral Investment Management: An Efficient Alternative to Modern Portfolio Theory* (McGraw-Hill Education, 2012), p. 53.

78   C. T. Howard, *Behavioral Portfolio Management: How successful investors master their emotions and build superior portfolios* (Harriman House, 2014), p. 20.

79   Marks, *The Most Important Thing*, p. 66.

80   Bernstein, *Against The Gods*, p. 197.

81   Taleb, *Antifragile*, p. 107.

82   P. DePodesta, 'Draft Review – About Process', itmightbedangerous. blogspot.com (June 10, 2008).

83   W. R. Gray, J. R. Vogel and D. P. Foulke, *DIY Financial Advisor: A Simple Solution to Build and Protect Your Wealth* (John Wiley & Sons, 2015), p. 31.

84   O'Shaughnessy, *What Works on Wall Street*, p. 42.

85   Portnoy, *The Investor's Paradox*, p. 43.

86   www.investopedia.com/terms/p/passivemanagement.asp

87   W. R. Gray and T. Carlisle, *Quantitative Value: A Practitioner's Guide to Automating Intelligent Investment and Eliminating Behavioral Errors* (John Wiley & Sons, 2012), p. 9.

88   A. M. Soe, 'SPIVA U.S. Scorecard', S&P Dow Jones Indices (2014).

89   Portnoy, *The Investor's Paradox*, pp. 54–55.

90   R. D. Arnott, J. C. Hsu, J. M. West, *The Fundamental Index: A Better Way to Invest* (John Wiley & Sons, 2008), p. 72.

91   J. Gittelsohn, 'End of Era: Passive Equity Funds Surpass Active in Epic Shift', Bloomberg (September 11, 2019).

92   A. Task, 'Pride cometh before the fall: Indexing edition', aarontask. tumblr.com (August 29, 2014).

93   J. Felder, 'Are Passive Investors Taking On Far More Risk Than They Realize?', thefelderreport.com (February 3, 2016).

94   Taleb, *Antifragile*, p. 5.

95   Arnott, Hsu, West, *The Fundamental Index*, p. 72.

96   R. D. Arnott, A. L. Berkin and J. Ye, 'How Well Have Taxable Investors Been Served in the 1980's and 1990's?', First Quadrant (2000).

97   B.G. Malkiel and C. Ellis, *The Elements of Investing: Easy Lessons for Every Investor* (John Wiley & Sons, 2013), p. 33.

98   Portnoy, *The Investor's Paradox*, p. 33.

99   J. Zweig, 'Behavioral Finance: What Good Is It, Anyway?', jasonzweig.com (June 20, 2015).

100   Lindstrom, *Buyology*, p. 158.

101   J. Montier, 'Painting by numbers: an ode to quant', DrKW Macro Research (August 2, 2006), p. 3.

102 Gray and Carlisle, *Quantitative Value*, p. 27.

103 Ibid.

104 Silver, *The Signal and the Noise*.

105 M.J. Mauboussin, *Think Twice: Harnessing the Power of Counterintuition* (Harvard Business Review Press, 2012), p. 44.

106 Carlson, *Common Sense*, p. 93.

107 Gray, Vogel and Foulke, *DIY Financial Advisor*, p. 23.

108 Mauboussin, *Think Twice*, p. 45.

109 N.N. Taleb, *Fooled By Randomness: The Hidden Role of Chance in Life and in the Markets* (Random House, 2005), p. xlvii.

110 T. Dinkelman, J. A. Levinsohn and R. Majelantle, 'When Knowledge Is Not Enough: HIV/AIDS Information and Risk Behavior in Botswana', NBER Working paper (2006).

111 B. Schwartz, *The Paradox of Choice: Why More Is Less* (Harper Perennial, 2005), p. 113.

112 Derman, *Models Behaving Badly*, p. 140.

113 Taleb, *Antifragile*, p. 190.

114 Schwartz, *The Paradox of Choice*, p. 75.

115 Antonacci, *Dual Momentum*, p. 34.

116 Graham and Zweig, *The Intelligent Investor*, pp. 39–40.

117 Silver, *The Signal and the Noise*, p. 185.

118 Carlson, *Common Sense*, p. xii.

119 Graham and Zweig, *The Intelligent Investor*, p. 31.

120 Marks, *The Most Important Thing*, p. 7.

121 R. Hargreaves, 'Seth Klarman: Now's Not The Time To Give Up On Value', valuewalk.com (January 26, 2016).

122 M. Cremers and A. Petajisto, 'How Active is Your Fund Manager? A New Measure That Predicts Performance' (SSRN, March 31, 2009).

123 D. Yanofsky, 'How you could have turned $1,000 into billions of dollars by perfectly trading the S&P 500 this year' qz.com (December 16, 2013).

124 Carlson, *Common Sense*, p. 66.

125 Malkiel, *Random Walk*, p. 161.

126 B. Casselman, 'Worried About The Stock Market? Whatever You Do, Don't Sell.', FiveThirtyEight.com (August 24, 2015).

127 Malkiel, *Random Walk*, p. 186.

128   M. T. Faber, 'A Quantitative Approach to Tactical Asset Allocation', SSRN (February 1, 2013).

129   E. Rosenbaum, '$128 billion and growing: Warren Buffett's Berkshire Hathaway cash puzzle', CNBC (November 1, 2019).

130   J. Felder, 'How To Time The Market Like Warren Buffett: Part 1', thefelderreport.com (August 7, 2014).

131   J. Felder, 'Don't Buy The Buy-And-Hold Line Of BS', thefelderreport.com (August 5, 2014).

132   'Trend Following In Financial Markets: A Comprehensive Backtest', philosophicaleconomics.com (January 2, 2016).

133   C.S. Asness, A. Ilmanen and T. Maloney, 'Market Timing Is Back In The Hunt For Investors', institutionalinvestor.com (November 11, 2015).

134   C. T. Howard, *The New Value Investing: How to Apply Behavioral Finance to Stock Valuation Techniques and Build a Winning Portfolio* (Harriman House, 2015), p. 9.

135   J. L. Evans and S. H. Archer, 'Diversification and the Reduction of Dispersion: An Empirical Analysis', *The Journal of Finance* 23:5 (December 1968).

136   J. Greenblatt, *You Can Be a Stock Market Genius: Uncover the Secret Hiding Places of Stock Market Profits* (Touchstone, 1999), p. 9.

137   Graham and Zweig, *The Intelligent Investor*, p. 114.

138   Howard, *New Value Investing*, p. 95.

139   Gray and Carlisle, *Quantitative Value*.

140   Montier, *Value Investing*, p. 37.

141   C. H. Browne, 'Value Investing and Behavioral Finance', presentation to Columbia Business School (November 15, 2000).

142   Widger and Crosby, *Personal Benchmark*, p. 232.

143   M. A. Jones, *Women of The Street: Why Female Money Managers Generate Higher Returns (and How You Can Too)* (Palgrave Macmillan, 2015), p. 278.

144   R. B. Cohen, C. Polk and B. Silli, 'Best Ideas', SSRN.com (March 15, 2010).

145   Silver, *The Signal and the Noise*, p. 237.

146   T. Griffin, 'A Dozen Things I've Learned from Marty Whitman/ Third Avenue about Investing', 25iq.com (December 15, 2013).

147 Lofton, *Warren Buffett Invests Like a Girl*, p. 86.

148 Gray and Carlisle, *Quantitative Value*, p. 16.

149 B. Shiv, 'Thinking Money – Horizontal Wine Tasting', YouTube. com (October 14, 2014).

150 Silver, *The Signal and the Noise*, p. 365.

151 R. J. Connors, *Warren Buffett on Business: Principles from the Sage of Omaha* (Wiley, 2009), p. 159.

152 Marks, *The Most Important Thing*, p. 33.

153 Ibid., pp. 46–47.

154 C. H. Browne, W. H. Browne, J. D. Spears, T. H. Shrager and R. Q. Wyckoff, Jr., 'What Has Worked In Investing: Studies of Investment Approaches and Characteristics Associated with Exceptional Returns' (Tweedy, Browne Company, revised edition, 2009).

155 Gray and Carlisle, *Quantitative Value*, p. 220.

156 J. Lakonishok, R.W. Vishny and A. Shleifer, 'Contrarian Investment, Extrapolation and Risk' (Working paper, 1993).

157 Montier, *Value Investing*, p. 75.

158 Lakonishok, Vishny and Shleifer, 'Contrarian Investment'.

159 R. Ibbotson, 'Decile Portfolios of the NYSE, 1967–1984', Yale School of Management Working Paper (1986).

160 E. F. Fama and K. R. French, 'The Cross-Section of Expected Stock Returns', *Journal of Finance* 47:2 (1992).

161 O'Shaughnessy, *What Works on Wall Street*, p. 85.

162 Lofton, *Warren Buffett Invests Like a Girl*, p. 71.

163 O'Shaughnessy, *What Works on Wall Street*, p. 127.

164 Montier, *Little Book of Behavioral Investing*.

165 Browne, 'What Has Worked In Investing' (revised edition, 2009).

166 en.wikipedia.org/wiki/Blockbuster_LLC

167 M. Graser, 'Epic Fail: How Blockbuster Could Have Owned Netflix', *Variety* (November 12, 2013).

168 Gray and Carlisle, *Quantitative Value*, p. 36.

169 Lofton, *Warren Buffett Invests Like a Girl*, p. 56.

170 T. Reed, 'Buffett Decries Airline Investing Even Though at Worst He Broke Even', *Forbes* (May 13, 2013).

171 Malkiel, *Random Walk*, p. 97.

172 Graham and Zweig, *The Intelligent Investor*, p. 304.

173 J.D. Piotroski, 'Value Investing: The Use of Historical Financial Statement Information to Separate Winners from Losers', University of Chicago Graduate School of Business (2002).

174 Ibid.

175 en.wikipedia.org/wiki/Joel_Greenblatt

176 S. Max, 'Writing a Bigger Book', *Barron's* (August 23, 2014).

177 'Magic Formula Investing – In 3 Steps', theintelligentinvestor.com (June 11, 2010).

178 S. Greenspan, 'Why We Keep Falling for Financial Scams', *The Wall Street Journal* (January 3, 2009).

179 Carlson, *Common Sense*, p. xiii.

180 Marks, *The Most Important Thing*.

181 Steenbarger, *Psychology of Trading*, p. 61.

182 J. Tierney, 'At Airports, a Misplaced Faith in Body Language', *The New York Times* (March 23, 2014).

183 C. F. Bond, Jr., and B. M. DePaulo, 'Accuracy of Deception Judgments', *Personality and Social Psychology Review* 10:3 (2006).

184 Tierney, 'At Airports'.

185 J. Montier, 'Seven Sins of Fund Management: A behavioural critique', DrKW Macro Research (November 2005).

186 S. Finkelstein, *Why Smart Executives Fail: And What You Can Learn from Their Mistakes* (Portfolio, 2004).

187 www.cfosurvey.org/about.html

188 J.R. Graham and C.R. Harvey, 'Expectations, optimism and overconfidence' (2005).

189 Statman, *What Investors Really Want*, p. 8.

190 D. Giamouridis, M. Liodakis and A. Moniz, 'Some Insiders are Indeed Smart Investors' (SSRN, July 29, 2008).

191 Browne, 'What Has Worked In Investing' (revised edition, 2009).

192 'Warren Buffett on Share Repurchases', *Value Investing World* (September 13, 2012).

193 C. J. Loomis, 'Beating the market by buying back stock', *Fortune* (November 21, 2012).

194 Gray and Carlisle, *Quantitative Value*, p. 168.

195 O'Shaughnessy, *What Works on Wall Street*, p. 189.

196 Carlson, *Common Sense*, p. 84.

197 C. H. Browne, W. H. Browne, J. D. Spears, T. H. Shrager and R. Q. Wyckoff, Jr., 'What Has Worked In Investing: Studies of Investment Approaches and Characteristics Associated with Exceptional Returns' (Tweedy, Browne Company, 1992).

198 Ibid.

199 Antonacci, *Dual Momentum*, p. 13.

200 Newfound Research, 'Two Centuries of Momentum' (www.thinknewfound.com/foundational-series/two-centuries-of-momentum).

201 Ibid.

202 Antonacci, *Dual Momentum*, p. 15.

203 Ibid., p. 16.

204 Newfound Research, 'Two Centuries of Momentum'.

205 W. E. Buffett, 'The Superinvestors of Graham-And-Doddsville' (1984).

206 N. Jegadeesh and S. Titman 'Returns to Buying Winners and Selling Losers: Implications for Stock Market Efficiency', *Journal of Finance* 48:1 (1993).

207 C. Geczy and M. Samonov, 'Two Centuries of Price Return Momentum', SSRN (2016).

208 B. Chabot, E. Ghysels and R. Jagannathan, 'Momentum Cycles and Limits to Arbitrage—Evidence from Victorian England and Post-Depression US Stock Markets', NBER working paper (2009).

209 C. S. Asness, A. Frazzini, R. Israel and T. J. Moskowitz, 'Fact, Fiction and Momentum Investing', SSRN (2014).

210 O'Shaughnessy, *What Works on Wall Street*, p. 408.

211 Ibid., p. 410.

212 Ibid., p. 419.

213 C. S. Asness, 'The Interaction of Value and Momentum Strategies', *Financial Analysts Journal* 53:2 (1997).

214 E. Derman, *Models.Behaving.Badly.: Why Confusing Illusion with Reality Can Lead to Disaster, on Wall Street and in Life* (Free Press, 2012), p. 48.

215 Ibid.

216 Gray and Carlisle, *Quantitative Value*, p. 29.

217 Graham and Zweig, *The Intelligent Investor*, p. 380.

218 J. M. Keynes, *The General Theory Of Employment, Interest, And Money* (CreateSpace, 2011), p. 93.
219 Zweig, 'Behavioral Finance: What Good Is It, Anyway?'.

Index

Note: Page numbers in *italic* refer to Figures; page numbers in **bold** refer to Tables; and page numbers in ***bold italic*** refer to Charts